A Helping Hand

Hand

with Children

by

Malcolm S. Southwood

A Helping Hand

Copyright 2000 by Monument, Ltd.

First Edition
First Printing, 2000

Cover design by Dana Cooper

ISBN 1-893657-02-7

Published by
The Healing Institute
RR#1 Box 286-C
Machias, ME 04654

Printed in the United States of America

DEDICATION

With love and thanks to
Susan, Ian, Paula and Adrian

THE AUTHOR

For over 20 years Malcolm Southwood has been helping people from all around the world with problems relating to health, happiness and spiritual awareness. He lectures regularly in America and Europe about the need to understand the child's individual needs as a beginning to understanding oneself. His common sense approach to understanding and helping people of all ages has caused him to be invited to lecture at schools, business conventions and health symposiums in many countries.

Mr. Southwood began writing in 1983. His works are in constant demand by people around the world and have been translated into several languages. Dedicated to raising awareness and understanding of oneself and others, he states his aims are to:

Return self-respect to those who have mislaid it,
Return independence to those who have lost it,
Return love to those who have forgotten it.

CONTENTS

INTRODUCTION

One of the most awesome responsibilities that we ever face is guiding our children through their early learning years, trying our best to help them become healthy, happy, productive, successful adults. Unfortunately, few parents realize that if a child's basic needs go unsatisfied (during the first ten to twelve years of life) the patterns of many future health problems become established in the subconscious. The disorders then lie dormant, in the recesses of the mind, waiting for the right circumstances to bring them to the surface.

There are certain trauma states that will nearly always cause a future negative affect on a child's health and happiness. Some may seem obvious but often it is a combination of traumas and always a child's personality type that decides the extent to which the dormant trauma will reappear later in the child's adult life.

For example, guilt on its own is unlikely to have a great affect on the child as he or she moves into the adult stage of life unless it is the sensitive personality and the guilt is associated with fear. In circumstances where first fear and then guilt are combined, conditions are set into place for a future phobia, especially in sensitive children. The type of phobia depends on personality type and is discussed later in the book.

Phobias can take many forms. The classic phobia of course is the unreasonable and uncontrollable fear of something that logically should cause no fear at all. What is often not realized is that unexplained adult pain can also be a phobia. The subconscious recreating the emotional or physical symptoms of the trauma to warn the adult of what it believes is impending danger. Again this is very much dependent upon personality type.

Preventive medicine is, of course, a good idea for all of us. We're smart to eat right, exercise, stop smoking, and the like. But taking preventive measures implies that you already have the problem inside you and are just trying to prevent it from coming out. It doesn't matter whether we talk about a heart attack, cancer, or multiple sclerosis, if the basis of that problem is already set up within the frame work of your personality it is only a matter of time before one of life's situations pulls the trigger.

Once we reach the age of emotional maturity the problem can be reversed only when we can access the groundwork of the disorder that was laid in our earlier years. By understanding our disorder, we can hold it in check. But we can't always reverse it.

So let's go back farther and protect our children from the conditions that will eventually produce health damaging symptoms. For this we need to have some understanding of personality types. Protective medicine only becomes a reality when we appreciate that one child's protective needs will be entirely different to another. This is based in the child's inherent personality. To protect our children's health we need to know their areas of sensitivity their attitudes, individual needs and emotional vulnerability.

A Helping Hand

Hand

with Children

A Helping Hand

CHAPTER 1

KNOWING YOUR CHILDREN

THE THREE PERSONALITY TYPES

I often hear parents saying proudly that they treated their children "equally" and loved all their children "the same." But how can that be right? All children are different; all have individual needs. Words that devastate one child will be disregarded by another. We are not the same and accept that certain adults react defensively to situations which others accept without question. We know that 'no two people are the same' so it can hardly come as any surprise that in guiding our children towards a healthy, happy and productive life each of them will need a different form of instruction, love and set of guide lines.

To know how to help them emotionally we first need a basic understanding of the different categories of personalities that our children are likely to fall into. The categories can be generalized into three types:

1)   Serious Children
2)   Fun-loving Children
3)   Passive Children

While children in each group may display some characteristics of the other two groups, their emotional needs will usually follow a predictable path as indicated by their basic classification. Once you have been able to establish and therefore understand the fundamental emotional personality of your child, you will be able to encourage and guide them according to their particular needs.

Personality needs fall into three main categories:

1) Physical Needs
2) Emotional Needs
3) Spiritual Needs.

The basic needs of the child are also the basic needs of the adult and you may be of a different category, or personality to your children. Therefore don't expect them to want what you want, appreciate the same things as you or even understand your reasoning or needs. If your child has the same basic personality as yourself you are lucky, at least you will understand them, but that doesn't mean you will have a close relationship. Their basic personality may not allow for this.

Don't expect your child to understand you. You can't put an old head on young shoulders. It is the parent who has to make the effort to understand the child and adjust their parenting style to fit the need. Our basic personality type determines which needs are most important to us.

Your child may be the serious, independent type in which case he/she will always display an independence of ideas. It doesn't mean they love or respect you less, they just have a need to be as independent as you probably do. It is knowing how to fulfill their need for independence while maintaining respect, love, understanding and family harmony that most parents find difficult. It's called

Love Them Their Way

PHYSICAL NEEDS: PERSONAL SPACE

The basic functioning need of all life is energy measured as a low pulsing electrical current which flows through every part of our body. This energy is enhanced with food, warmth, and shelter.

It is also essential that every child has personal space, even if that space is only a bed in the corner of a room. Even a dog needs its basket; and children are no less in need of their own space, a place where they can cry, hide, imagine, and develop deep within themselves without the disturbing energies of others invading their personal territory.

Don't give your child their own bed or room to then take it away when someone comes to visit. Serious Children particularly react against this invasion of privacy, they need their silent times. It creates anger, rebellion, and even destructive habits as they try to remove from their lives the invasive energies, which they feel are "in their space." Denial of personal space causes physical stress in people of all ages, bringing with it a variety of health problems. Your children are more sensitive than you are to the energy patterns of others and like to create their own environment in their own space. Your energy pattern is different to your child's, and to maintain their individual personality and energy frequency your child will need a place to escape to. Don't make the mistake of interpreting this as hostility towards you or other members of the family. They are just a different personality type which is reflected in the differing energy patterns between you.

Respect children's individual needs and they will respect yours

EMOTIONAL NEEDS: A VERY HUMAN NECESSITY

Emotional expression is a very human necessity and with it develops self-esteem, companionship, communication, and acknowledgment. If parents prohibit a child's emotional expression, the child will be withdrawn and lacking in self-worth or express overly emotional and attention-seeking behavior.

The children who are most affected by not being able to express themselves are the Fun-loving Children. Just as the Serious child needs to withdraw from time to time to know itself and reestablish an inner connectedness, so the child who is full of fun will need to move into your space, your energy field to express itself. This is a difficult personality to understand, especially as they begin to mature because they seem to have no need of a personal space and are unable to understand your need for one. It becomes more difficult when other children in the family are different and not being old enough to understand their siblings need for personal space the Fun-loving personality will often walk all over it, making family harmony difficult to achieve or maintain.

The loving parent will need to understand this child's need to invade and live in their energy for long periods of time. This child needs the energy of others to survive as a thriving and self assured personality. If parents restrict the need for emotional expression of such children, they will develop into rejection personalities with a whole host of psychosomatic health problems later in life.

There is no such thing as personal space to an emotional child, they own it all

SPIRITUAL NEEDS: PURPOSE IN LIFE

The third basic need has to do with purpose, achievement, and love. Of course, all three types need love and a sense of achievement in order to go on to a satisfying and happy life; but where the Serious child and the Fun-loving child can find these elements for themselves, the Passive child needs to obtain it from others.

Passive Children need a sense of fulfillment; they need to serve. They need to be brought up in an atmosphere that will not dampen their need to express love and feel loved. If denied love and the opportunity to show love in service to others, these children will soon lose their feeling of self-worth. Passive Children have a deep inner need to be needed; and when allowed to be of use, they exhibit all the loving qualities of their spiritual nature.

Spiritual love is not what you do, it is who you are.

INDIVIDUALIZING YOUR LOVE

Ensuring that your child's basic needs for growth, expression, and self-worth are satisfied is an essential part of parenting. If these needs are attended to, your children will grow to maximize their individual potential, thus achieving happiness, success and they will avoid most health problems. However, if children of all three types are treated equally, they will be prone to personality and health problems.

These difficulties are entirely predictable, based on the way a child is guided and loved during the formative years. If the basic needs are met at the beginning, the child will benefit throughout life. If not, at some stage health and happiness will break down.

Of course, all children need love, but surprisingly to many, they need to have it presented to them in different ways. All children need to be guided, and at times disciplined, but the guidance and discipline used in directing children to a fulfilling life must vary according to their basic personality.

No one is totally of one character type. We are a mixture of all the three types of personalities. For example, someone might be sixty percent Fun-loving, thirty percent Serious and ten percent Passive. Nevertheless, it is the main character in our personality that controls our reactions to life's varying situations. The categories listed below are guidelines, nothing more. You, the parent, using a lot of common sense and love are the best guide to your child's needs. No one can know them as intuitively as you do. Therapists, child counselors and people like me can only offer advice and guide lines. After all, you have your child's interests in your love and that is the most important factor in all parenting. The child needs to know

I was loved my way.

Reminders
Knowing Your Children

Don't expect your child to understand you.

Don't give your child a bed or room only to take it away when someone comes to visit.

Respect your child's individual needs and they will respect yours.

Children want to be loved their way.

Spiritual love is not what you do, it is who you are.

CHAPTER 2

THE SERIOUS CHILD:
Fighting the Fear of Failure

HARD WORKERS

To many of you it must seem wonderful to have studious, clever children who study hard and are always trying their best to succeed. If your children are like this, you know how hard they work and how they are always trying to get the best results. You also know that, unfortunately, they sometimes overdo it. They study and compete to a point where they lose a balanced perspective on life.

These Serious Children are naturally competitive; and if for some reason they fail their own high standards, they can become very upset. This situation is made many times worse if they are unlucky enough to have parents who are too ambitious for them.

Can you imagine the pressure these youngsters are put under by parents, who thinking they are doing the best for their children, push them to try even harder than they already are? I know that the parents' intentions are good; but when we push

Serious Children beyond their natural potential, they develop a fear of failure. Instead of enjoying life and their successes, they begin to worry about the results. It then becomes a fear of failure that drives them rather than a sense of enjoyment in what they are doing. When a Serious Child is pressured to succeed, the fear of failure grows in their subconscious and creates stress levels that make it impossible to relax. This fear of failure will become a permanent personality feature, which will persist throughout life.

Serious Children need to be encouraged to relax rather than pressured to do better. I always think it's helpful to encourage them to get involved in activities at which they're not naturally gifted. Let's be honest with ourselves, children who have a natural ability for math, for example, are not going to learn anything from doing more equations that will add to their character or broaden their perspectives on life. But if motivated to take an interest in some study or activity that does not come so easily, they will accept how it feels to be less than perfect and not worry about it. If Serious Children are encouraged to do only what can be achieved effortlessly, any performance below their self-expectations will cause them to feel like failures. It will cause them to have closed minds about what they don't understand.

These studious Serious Children need to learn how to be tolerant of themselves and their results, and so do their parents. If parents cannot tolerate failure by their children to measure up perfectly to their own high standards, these hard-working, dedicated youngsters will create levels of stress within their still-growing bodies; and in adult years this stress will become heart disease, stomach problems, and a host of other illnesses well known to be stress-related.

A Serious Child should never be asked or expected to produce results that are at the limit of his or her natural abilities.

NEVER GOOD ENOUGH

Never boast about a Serious Child's performance publicly, especially in front of the child, this is one of the worst things a parent can do. When little Suzy or Johnnie hear you telling your friends how clever they were on this or that exam or that they're going to get straight A's, they feel pressured to achieve to satisfy you, not themselves. This creates a need within them to always do better. Whatever level of achievement they reach, it will never be good enough.

Let Johnnie or Suzy achieve to their own levels, not yours. To expect your children to do well so you feel proud talking about them is asking *them* to fuel *your* ego. Why can't parents be content knowing they have happy, healthy, loving children? Why do these young people have to produce certain results before a parent can feel proud of them? Not all parents are like this, I know, but for many, as soon as they realize that they have gifted children, pride becomes synonymous with results. The child is then criticized at home for not doing better. This leads the child to believe that the praise given in public is not justified and praise so given will be taken away immediately when he or she gets home. They then come to detest praise knowing that it is going to lead to pressure and criticism at a later date.

If the child is unable to achieve to the parent's expectations,
it is the parent who is failing the child,
not the child who is failing the parent.

PUTTING YOURSELF IN YOUR CHILD'S SHOES

Once at one of my meetings, a woman stood up and said, "Are you telling me that when my child comes home from school, and her reports and school work show she could do better, I shouldn't bother about it? I shouldn't be concerned? Are you really saying that I shouldn't reprimand her in some way? That I'm wrong when I say, 'Come on, you can do better than that?' That I'm wrong to withhold some of her privileges until she starts to work harder and try harder?"

I could feel everybody in the room agreeing with her, that the daughter needed guidance and discipline to bring her back into line. After all, life is about competing; and without good results, she isn't going to get into the right college.

But think about this for a minute, as I suggested to the well-intentioned lady. Let's say you've had a bad day. You've just heard that your best friend is saying things about you that are untrue. The bank has sent a letter saying you are over your credit limit, again. You have a cold and are not feeling well, and you are worried that your husband might lose his job. You know what I mean; it's just been a *bad* day. Your husband comes home from work and notices that the dinner isn't ready, the house isn't dusted, and the morning papers haven't been put away. He says to you, "You can do better than this. You aren't trying hard enough, so I'm going to reduce your allowance until you put more effort into your work and improve your results."

Are you going to stand there meekly with your head bowed, clasping your hands behind your back, and say, "Sorry, I'll try harder tomorrow?"

I doubt it. And judging by the response that came from the audience neither would any other adult. You would quickly tell the husband what he could do with his ideas. But your children can't say these things, even though they have such thoughts, and so the pressure builds and they begin to fear you and their results. Children have worries and problems the same as adults do.

Wouldn't it be better instead to put an arm around your son or daughter and say, "What's wrong? Got a problem? Anything I can help with?" If your children are not succeeding or grades are dropping ask, "What's the problem?" If you have been doing this since they were little, they'll confide in you. And if they don't confide in you, it's your fault, not theirs. You've lost the balance between happiness and success and your child has become scared of you.

I know that sounds hard on caring, loving parents who only want the best for their children, but I'm on the side of the child in such circumstances every time. Serious Children need confidence and approval more than the other types do. They are critical enough of their own efforts without parents and teachers adding to it.

If you have Serious Children, do not drive these boys and girls to full potential. They will do it themselves. Let them find their own level of comfort as they begin to study and develop. Allow them to find their own balance in life between success and happiness instead of forcing them to view life as a balance between success and failure. Any intolerance of themselves leads to intolerance of others. Since Serious Children are not allowed to fail, they cannot abide failure or less than total effort by others especially as they get older.

> *Children who are in fear of their results are in fear of an adult*
> *Let it not be you.*

DESTROYING SELF-RESPECT

Very few parents realize that it is their casual remarks that determine their child's future attitude. The following are just a few of the many comments that destroy confidence and happiness in the Serious Child (children of the other two groups are less affected by the same statements):

"You should know that!" said when a little one comes asking for help or advice. If children ask a question when the answer is obvious, they are insecure in some area of their happiness and are asking for help. Listen to your children when they ask for help. A question may be a cover for a deeper problem, or it could be testing your current mood or attitude. Your answering, "You should know that!" prevents a child from going any further in confiding in you. "You didn't try hard enough!" or "Is that the best you can do?" spoken when he or she didn't get the highest score (or the score you wanted) on an exam, these comments, especially when repeated over the years, go toward creating a base of insecurity.

"That's not good enough." By whose standards isn't it good enough? If you are trying to force a Serious Child to meet your expectations, then this child has become a status symbol in your life and interprets these remarks to mean: "To be loved, I have to succeed to the level of my parents expectations of me." What a terrible thought to have to grow up with! Situations become even worse when no matter what a Serious Child does, it just is *never* good enough. Imagine, for example, what goes through the mind of a child who goes home with ninety-nine percent on a test, feeling happy and accomplished, and someone asks, "What happened to the other one percent?"

I recall one young man who won a scholarship when he shared first place in the finals. His father's only comment was, "Why didn't you get it all?" That one sentence haunted him for the rest of his life. It stripped him of any satisfaction he might enjoy from his obvious achievements. He felt like a failure because he didn't "get it all."

"Wow! What a great result!" isn't really so hard to say, is it? This reminds me of a little girl named Janie and the time when she went home feeling pleased with an exam score of eighty percent, which was better than she'd gotten before. Instead of saying: "That's wonderful; I'm proud of you," her mother's only response was, "What did the other kids do?" After hearing this remark, Janie had to admit she's only average. In one smart sentence, her self-respect and happiness were swept away. Does it matter what other kids do? This is your child.

Children need your love, not persecution.

I remember consoling one boy because the only praise he got for a good grade was, "It must have been an easy test."

As if these comments were not enough to destroy confidence and self-respect, and breed a fear of failure, the one that really causes the high achiever to self-destruct is, "You will never be as good as your father, mother, sister, brother, etc." This is positive programming for low expectations. Boys and girls to whom this is said will know that no matter how hard they try, they'll always be a failure in the minds of those they love and want to be loved by. The strange thing is that a Serious Child will then try even harder to extract some praise from the situation. But such praise, such love, never comes; and so the fear of failure becomes ever more deeply embedded.

The more assertive Serious Child with pushy, hypercritical parents will become introverted and sometimes aggressive. In a sort of protective mode, such children go through life ignoring, distrusting, or belittling what they don't understand or achieve. They are often very logical and will put aside anything that does not fit into their neatly ordered view of life.

As adults, they are often lonely and fear criticism that they sometimes overcome by ruthlessness, ambition, boasting, and the pursuit of power. Unable to accept failure in any realm of their lives, these unhappy people always hear, deep in their hearts, the words of parents or teachers who did so much to encourage them with comments like, "You can do better than that!" and "What happened to the other one percent?"

And so the children who began life wanting to do well and please everybody finish up believing they are pleasing no one. Success, therefore, becomes failure. And eventually, stress-related health problems overwhelm their lives.

The Serious Child rarely enjoys success as an adult, regardless of personal accomplishments and career achievements. For all time, they are haunted by the familiar criticism: "Is that the best you can do?"

Serious Children try to please through their efforts and results.
They find their happiness in approval.
Their loneliness in criticism.

LEARNING EMOTION

Can high achievers, the Serious Children, be protected from stress-related illnesses? I believe they can by being better prepared to manage their natural abilities, whether intellectual, physical, or creative.

Serious Children need space in their lives; they need a place they can call their own, a bedroom, a den, and a play area free of other peoples' vibrations. If your serious-type daughter's refuge is her bed, for example, you will create all sorts of emotional difficulties if you ask her to give it up when friends visit. To this child *her* space is sacrosanct.

Serious Children are logical and orderly in their thinking, and these traits are reflected in the tidiness of their space. In their own domain, they are usually neat and know exactly where everything is. They will often shut themselves away in their room, and they do not react kindly to siblings invading their territory.

Serious Children sometimes have difficulty being emotional. Emotion for them is a learned experience, not a natural response to a situation and, therefore, they are very controlled in what they do, say, or think. Often, these serious types find it difficult to be spontaneous in response to life's daily challenges. For them spontaneity is a learned experience; so if you have Serious Children, teaching them how to hug and love, letting them know that it is okay to cry or come to you with problems, will all be part of your responsibilities. Serious Children who are born to parents who themselves are unemotional will not learn how to share their emotions with others. They will be withdrawn and rarely experience the joy of loving and sharing emotionally. Because they do not fully enter into or understand emotion the Serious child matures to be very in control of their own lives. They will not allow any other to control their lives except of course their parents and teachers and only while they are young. Once free, and in charge of their own destiny, they take full control of their lives, as if refusing to allow anyone to criticize them again. But as children they were taught how to do that for themselves.

As they grow older, the high achievers interfere in no one else's life, and tolerate no interference in their own lives. As such, they become very private people with a tendency to brood rather than to ask for help. Always in their mind are the parents words, 'You should know that.'

The Serious Child will never forget your disparaging words "You should know that."

A PRICE TO BE PAID

Most Serious Children suffer stress-related illnesses as adults. Fear of failure forces the child, the adolescent, and finally the adult to try to achieve beyond their full potential, leaving themselves no room for anything less than total success. Many parents will expect nothing less from their children. But children are not robots. Life is about happiness not competitive success, and in spite of what you may believe the two are not related. If they are, then the vast majority of people must be terribly unhappy.

Serious Children whose fear of failure is not allayed by understanding and encouragement are headed straight for the classic coronary diseases: blocked arteries and heart attacks. Less serious body language, but still on the list of potential illnesses for the fear-of-failure types, are gastrointestinal problems like ulcers and irritable bowel syndrome. Also, as a result of not being sufficiently relaxed, they are subject to sports injuries, such as strained back and shoulder muscles and damaged joints.

While Serious Children are often dedicated to their studies, they're not simply bookworms that never see the light of day. The fear of failure can drive these youngsters to high achievement in other areas, too, including athletics.

But even though they can run fast and jump and swim and play ball, they are prone to injuries like torn tendons, pulled ligaments, and twisted ankles. They are not supple. They're so stressed-out that their muscles are tight.

As in other areas, parents must not push their Serious Children to be overachievers in sports. And they especially must not prod them toward careers as professional athletes.

As adults, these people often exercise daily and take mouthfuls of vitamins and minerals to prevent the problems they know they are prone to. But although preventive medicine may help, it is not the answer. It is their inner drive and subconscious programming which are all messed up. Although their health problems appear to be a result of the way they live, the way they live is controlled by the way their subconscious was programmed many years earlier. Most of their illnesses would be avoided if these logically thinking, self-demanding characters could reprogram their subconscious computer.

Unfortunately, because of their completely logical way of analyzing everything, the Serious avoid anything to do with the unexplained and mystical art of healing. Only when healing can be described logically will they consider trying to have the causes of their stress removed. If they come for healing, it is usually because of a physical problem such as a strained muscle, although it is the emotional release these people are most in need of. Without it, the subconscious fear of failure drives them on until they collapse.

Pills, drugs, and/or surgery might deal effectively with their symptoms; but the underlying cause remains, and the subconscious will maintain its mastery of these Serious-type people. They will suffer from physical illnesses brought on by an over-demanding, never-satisfied subconscious, which mirrors the parent(s) who trained it.

Fear of failure causes injury problems for the serious sportsman
Unable to relax, muscles and joints strain more easily.

THE INTELLECTUAL LADDER

When it comes to choosing schools for children, all parents naturally want the best education they can afford and to which their children can gain entry. It seems as though the only criterion parents consider today when evaluating schools is the number of high achievers they each turn out. This may not be the best way to choose your child's educational program. Just as all three types of children have different parenting needs, so they also have different social and educational needs.

Children usually spend the early grades in a small, local school. Since Serious Children want to achieve recognition early, it is possible during these first few years that they have never been out of the top three in their class. So when they move to a larger school, one with a reputation for top results, they find themselves among similar high achievers; and the pressure to uphold their level is increased tenfold. As they move up the intellectual ladder, the pressure builds; and although they probably don't display many signs of stress, the fear of failure is real for them, especially if they have demanding parents.

The anxiety many students endure in order to satisfy the ambitions of parents or teachers threatens their health. It is no wonder they fall victim to stress-related disorders in later years, when all the tension accumulated during the adolescent years finally causes the system to overload in the adult.

Sad to say, some don't survive even that long. I recall one

student who, after completing his entrance exams to a university in the U.K., was sure he had not done well enough to satisfy his father. The pressure became so great that rather than face his father as a failure, he committed suicide a few days before the results were posted. He'd gotten straight A's.

The fear of failure can be a killer.

Fear of failure destroys happiness first, then health.

It is a parent's responsibility to protect children from pressure, not add to it. To force them to achieve at maximum effort for 15 years is unnatural; a price will be paid in future years. Preventive medicine might be helpful, but it will not undo the damage done in earlier years. Serious Children should not be sent to the best schools; they will perform just as well in a less competitive environment. These achievers push themselves without the added pressure of vying for honors with other high-powered students or of being held responsible for maintaining their school's reputation.

I have spent many hours counseling youngsters of all ages whose parents and/or teachers thought they weren't trying hard enough. I usually spend the time teaching the child or adolescent how to deal with the adult who is causing the problem. This approach is often far more effective than dealing with the imagined attitude problems of the child. Children haven't been taught how to deal with demanding adults any more than adults have been taught how to help serious, studious youngsters. I've discovered that children learn faster than parents or teachers; and once children recognize the difficulties adults have in understanding their needs, they will adjust to manage the adults. And thus, they overcome the pressure and begin to enjoy the process of learning.

Enroll Serious Children in schools or colleges with fewer high achievers. This way, you will reduce the pressure brought about by the fear of failure and allow them time to enjoy the company of their peers, instead of seeing them as competition. Choose a school where your Serious Child will succeed easily and be happy without worrying about the caliber of the other students, not one where there will be pressure to maintain the school's reputation. In such an environment, the serious types will be able to set their own standards of excellence. The lowered level of stress will pay dividends for years to come in the form of better health and happiness.

Serious Children respond better when they are not constantly being compared to others.
They need to hear words of approval, not criticism.

A STUDY IN HEALING: A SLAVE TO HIS INTELLIGENCE?

I have a friend whose ambitious son has an IQ of over 170. At the age of twelve he wrote to an impressive international company regarding its career-advancement program. After the company reviewed the boy's excellent academic records and recognized his potential, they offered him a full scholarship straight through college. He accepted.

Half way through college, the boy returned home and told his father he had changed his mind and now wanted to be an artist.

"Then be an artist!" his father said.

"But Dad, it's causing problems with my professor. He says that half the students at school would give their right arm to have the advantages, the academic ability, and the promise that I have. It would be a waste of my intelligence."

At that point, my friend stopped his son and said, "Are you going to be a slave to your intelligence for the rest of your life? Or, are you going to use it to make you happy?"

"Thanks, Dad "

The boy went on to a flourishing career as an artist. He did not become a famous scientist with a prestigious title and a fat paycheck; but he is happy and healthy, and his parents are no less proud of him.

It's important to avoid pressuring youngsters to enter a career within their ability but not to their liking. Likewise, they should not enter a field to which they're not suited. Sometimes, a child will ask questions like those posed by the young man above just to test the attitude of their parents. I know of one young woman who, after her parents gave her the choice of switching courses of study, stayed with the same subjects as before. After presenting the dilemma to her parents, she felt that she had gained their support to set her own standards and that she would not be working diligently simply because they expected her to.

There's little chance of heart attacks in adult life for these two students.

A parent has a duty to recognize shifts in a child's preferences and with love, encourage them to search for their own direction in life.

A STUDY IN HEALING: A SECRET ENGINEER

A boy called Tom, who was fourteen, came with his mother to see if I could do anything about his condition. It was a condition in which the blood, for some unknown reason, was not flowing to the knees, with the result that the kneecaps were not growing. In fact, they were beginning to flake and break up. This is how it was described to me by his mother. He had seen a medical specialist just a week or so earlier and been told that there was nothing that could be done, as it was a condition, not a disease, but that maybe when he had finished growing all might come out right.

The condition was very painful, and Tom wasn't able to straighten his legs properly. Obviously, any form of sport was out of the question. I sat him down in front of me and held his ankles to harmonize with his energy. I do this to "tune in" to people's subconscious thoughts. It took only a few minutes to realize why this condition had come about.

Tom was a natural sportsman—excellent at swimming, football, gymnastics, golf, and, I suppose, anything else he cared to try his hand at. He had decided at a very early age that sports would be his career. He planned to go on to college and qualify as a gym teacher. So I asked him what he wanted to do. That might sound like a silly question, but it had the desired effect. He didn't answer. I asked him again. Still no answer. Then I asked him what he wanted to do *now* and straight away he said, "Engineering."

When Tom changed his mind, as youngsters do, and began to feel that he no longer wanted to make his career in athletics, there shouldn't have been any difficulty. But if you are gifted and everyone is expecting great things of you, it is difficult to disappoint people, especially if you are sensitive and don't wish to hurt anyone. His parents had put a lot of time and energy into helping him to achieve what had been his ambition, with extra lessons, trips to sports gatherings, etc. His coach at school had also given up his weekends and evenings to train Tom. Many people had done a lot to help Tom in his ambitions; and when those ambitions changed, he just didn't know how to tell them.

It was then that his subconscious controller took over. Recognizing Tom's dilemma, the controller decided to reduce the blood supply to the knees, knowing very well what the outcome would be. It wasn't very long before Tom was in acute pain and unable to take part in any sport.

After I had explained all this to Tom, I took his ankles and held his legs straight out in front of him. His pain had practically gone, and his legs were almost straight. His mother was astounded. In less than half an hour, Tom was more or less back to normal. Of course, it would take a little while for his knees to heal, but otherwise his condition was cured. Why? Quite simply because Tom's controller knew that now his mother knew of his changed ambitions, there would be no need to cause a malfunction in his knees. A visit to the doctor three weeks later confirmed that Tom's knees were healing fast and no treatment would be necessary.

A child is not a status symbol.
They are spirits of love looking to you to guide them towards happiness.

Reminders
Serious Children

Serious children are prone to fear of failure

If your children don't confide in you it's your fault, not theirs.

Instead of criticizing when they get it wrong, why not ask, 'got a problem?' 'Can I help?'

Let them achieve to their own level, not yours.

Don't pressure the Serious child to do well to fuel your ego.

If you praise your children in public and criticize them in private they will come to detest praise from anyone.

Teach your serious children how to relax in preference to encouraging them to work even harder.

Serious children should never be asked or expected to produce results that are at the limit of their natural abilities.

Let your child achieve to their own levels of success, not yours.

When praise equals pressure, the parent is failing the child.

Serious children need confidence and approval more than other types.

Children who are in fear of their results are in fear of an adult.

Children need your love, not persecution.

Never, never say, 'you can do better than that'. They did the best they could at the time.

Children find happiness in approval and loneliness in criticism.

To the serious child personal space is sacrosanct.

Serious children do not like being told what to do.

Fear of failure destroys happiness first, then health.

Serious children have long memories and never forget your disparaging words.

It is a parent's responsibility to protect children from pressure, not add to it.

Children don't know how to deal with demanding adults.

A parent has a duty to recognize shifts in a child's preferences.

With love children should be encouraged to search for their own direction in life.

Children are not status symbols. They are spirits of love looking to you to guide them toward happiness.

CHAPTER 3

THE FUN-LOVING CHILD:
Living With the Fear of Rejection

EXTROVERTS

If you have children who are full of fun and have boundless energy, you're probably stressed out trying to keep up with them. Having happy Fun-loving Children must seem like the answer to every parent's dream; but once they get past the early years the demands some of these children make on time and energy can be exhausting. These children crave attention, friendship, and love. The problem for them is that the more they crave it, the more other children and adults avoid them.

These extroverts demand activity, and if there isn't any, they will soon create some. They dislike quiet activities such as reading, writing, or listening to music. To this type of personality, *quiet* is an unknown word. They burst into the room disturbing the peace as they demand everybody's attention. Unfortunately for them, they are insensitive to the needs of their less boisterous siblings and friends, and so they quickly become unpopular both at home and at school. The more a child is of this character, the less popular he or she will be and rejection becomes an issue in their lives. They grow to have a fear of rejection.

LET'S BAKE A CAKE

Fun-loving children know all about rejection, for they have experienced it since an early age. All through life, their exuberance is unstoppable, and it is their boundless energy and constant activity that others try to avoid. For example, if Mother is making a cake, the Fun-loving child will demand to be involved and will enjoy every minute of it. This little character will be up to the elbows in flour and act as if the whole process were one big game and not something to be taken seriously. Soon, there will be cake batter up the walls, on the floor, and all over the clothes. This child will love having a wonderful time "helping"; but when the fun part is over, the little whirlwind will run off to play or annoy someone else, without a second thought about helping to clean up the mess. Parental scolding or shouting will do no good. To Fun-loving Children, life is one big game and that's why they are subject to rejection.

The Fun-loving Child seems to know when rejection is imminent. As a result, these children try everything they can think of to make others happy, attempting to be accepted. They do not understand that not everyone is as full of energy as they are; and the more they are rejected, the more demanding they become.

Fun-loving Children have a need to be noticed. Even in ill health they are unable to quiet down and seem to live through all kinds of sickness, as if nothing had ever been wrong.

The demands the Fun-loving Child makes upon others
are endless.

A GAME AT THE AIRPORT

The depth of Fun-loving Children's fear of rejection will depend upon the patience and love of others. Facing continual rejection, this personality will develop strategies to test for disapproval, especially as they get older.

Fun-loving types often feed on other peoples' energy, which is another reason why they are often unpopular. Other children push them away, not wanting them around. Because parents do not always have limitless amounts of time to give, Fun-loving Children develop ways to attract a parent's attention in order to ensure that the adult's energy is focused on them.

I remember sitting in an airport lounge and watching a fascinating mind game played among a Fun-loving little girl about five years old, her seven-year-old brother, and their mother. The little girl was on one side of the mother and her brother on the other. Quiet and requiring no attention, the little boy was reading books. Even at this age, it was obvious he was a Serious Child but, the little girl was full of energy. She wouldn't sit still; and to keep her mother's attention and, therefore, to keep energy focused on her self, she asked question after question. She kept dropping her toys on the floor, and her mother kept picking them up. In order to attend to the nonstop demands of her daughter, the mother turned her back on her little boy.

After a while, when the little girl was trying to gain the attention of one of the other passengers in the airport, her mother was able to turn her attention to her little boy; and she started to read with him. The girl, seeking to regain her mother's attention, dropped her toys on the floor. But when she didn't get the response she wanted, she very deliberately got off her chair, gathered up all her toys, went to the other side of her mother, dropped her toys on her mother's lap; and squeezed herself between her brother and her mother. She had won her mother's attention back. The little boy continued to read on his own, but the sideways look he gave his younger sister said it all. He was already beginning to instinctively dislike his sister. A rejection she would soon come to know and fear.

During all this time, the mother was quietly unaware of the drama being played out between her children and herself. She had no idea her five- year- old daughter was controlling her. Control is an enormous factor in the personality of Fun-loving Children.

Fun-loving Children try to control everybody's lives, and they are good at it. That is another reason why they are rejected.

NO NEED FOR PRIVACY

Fun-loving Children do not respect another person's space. Personal space has no meaning to them, for they are comfortable anywhere and everywhere, and are open to anyone who wants to come into their space. When these children invade the sanctity and peace of another's space, they won't even realize it. This is an irritation to those who jealously guard their personal space, which can be anything from a bedroom, a car, or a home. With no desire for privacy, the Fun-loving extrovert cannot understand why others should need it. This character is totally unselfish, having no need to hold to themselves their own energy with 'things' in the way the serious types do. This is yet one more aspect of the Fun-loving personality that brings on rejection.

***Even normally tolerant people reject
the Fun-loving types who overwhelm them.***

EXASPERATION, THEN REJECTION

The Fun-loving Child is probably the most undisciplined and untidy child around. His or her bedroom is always a shambles. They drop clothing where they take them off, leaving a trail from door to bed as they undress. Their untidy lifestyle, the way they leave everything out and rarely put anything away, is a reflection of their mind. All thoughts are out in the open for everyone to see. They have no secrets and are usually quite incapable of keeping one.

Fun-loving children are continually being rejected, more out of exasperation than anything else. Although they are usually much loved, parents, teachers, and others quickly come to regard them as a nuisance. As a result, their attempts to attract attention create just the opposite effect, attracting only comments trying to shoo them away. "Not now, I'm busy." or "Oh no, not you again!" "Go ask someone else. Can't you see I'm busy?" "Be quiet!" The list is endless.

When exposed to such constant rejection from the adults around them, Fun-loving children come to expect it. But that doesn't make the rejection any easier to bear; and with every negative remark, with every instance of rejection, the hurt goes a little bit deeper until, over time, these children are programmed to expect rejection in all avenues of life. And soon, they begin to seek it out. For example, when making appointments, they will want the time that is not available, an hour when the office is closed, a day when where there are no openings on the schedule. This sort of behavior suits two purposes: one, it generates attention, and two it sets up a test to see if the expectation of rejection will be met.

Fun-loving children need the attention of others.
It is their life force.

LAUGHING AND SULKING

As children, Fun-loving types rarely show that they have been hurt or rejected, and they usually laugh their way through a painful situation. Just as the Serious Child will become more assertive when pressured, the Fun-loving Child will become more demanding when ignored. You cannot put youngsters of this personality down; if something upsets them, they will soon bounce back.

Although quickly accustomed to rejection, on occasions when the hurt is severe, the normally cheerful demeanor of Fun-loving Children will disappear; they will tend to sulk. They may slink off into their own room and ignore everyone or simply look wounded while wandering around the house without a word. Such taciturn behavior is so unusual that it is not long before a parent, grandparent, sister, or brother is trying to make them happy; and so sulking has fulfilled its purpose in attracting the needed attention. A Fun-loving Child learns to control the members of the family at an early age.

*Fun-loving Children demand attention
and see rejection where there is none.*

LOVING BIG, BUT NOT DEEP

As adults, the rejected Fun-loving Children can be difficult to deal with. They go to extremes as they try to gain attention and tend to wear clothes others within their social group find strange or inappropriate. Life's actors, they love the spotlight, but their flamboyant and demonstrative ways can be wearing on those around them. They need an outlet for their abundant love of life. Otherwise, they become depressed and angry. If they have a serious side to their nature, they will turn their energy into running a business or some other activity.

This exuberant and explosive personality is full of energy and rarely feels emotionally down. Often, Fun-loving types will indulge in exaggeration to make themselves sound better or worse, depending upon the result they want to achieve. Passive and Serious Children resent the overstatement and nonstop energy of the Fun-loving Child. This is why most Fun-loving Children find it so hard to make and keep friends; often, they grow up not trusting in any relationship, because they have been rejected too many times to trust in the affections or attention of others. When they fall in love, they go overboard with the outward expression of their feelings. Yet, anticipating rejection, they rarely allow their feelings to go deep, for fear of being hurt, rendering them quite capable of loving more than one person at a time.

Some times Happy children need to be asked with love
'Are you happy?"

EVERY ILLNESS YOU CAN IMAGINE

These vividly emotional people can suffer with every sort

of physical illness you can imagine. But in the accepted medical sense, nothing is wrong with them. Doctors will try every sort of treatment possible, applying even the most high-tech procedures, without success, for Fun-loving patients, due to the subconscious intensity of their emotions, have transformed a worry or an anxiety into a physical illness or disability. This personality suffers mostly from psychosomatic disorders, health problems that are under the control of their subconscious and that can disappear as quickly as they arose.

Fun-loving people usually refuse to be unhappy, at least for very long, unless something triggers their earlier childhood rejections. Then they are capable of uncontrollable emotional outbursts.

When anxieties are not allowed emotional release,
the subconscious finds another outlet for
them in the body language of physical disability.

I have seen this personality with cancer; and if the anxiety or emotion causing the illness is released through healing, the patient will recover instantly. Of course, not all instant healings take place because the patient has a Fun-loving personality; any more than all Fun-loving people undergo psychosomatic illnesses. But when a person with a rejection personality believes he or she has been accepted, it is surprising how quickly they will recover. Unfortunately, this person is just as likely to fall ill again with some other condition if by doing so, they can feed their need for acceptance.

Parents of any attention-seeking child should be most careful to avoid any action or comment that could be interpreted as rejection. No child likes to feel rejected or unloved, but the Fun-loving Child will see rejection where there is none. And when there is real rejection, the Fun-loving Child takes it to heart.

A STUDY IN HEALING: IT ISN'T RIGHT!

I knew Elizabeth was a rejection character even before I saw her because she wouldn't accept any appointment we offered her. When she finally arrived in my office, she told me that she'd lost the sight in her left eye. "It isn't right!" she said to me just after she sat down in my healing room. "It isn't right."

"What isn't right?"

"I've been left! It isn't right. It isn't right. I don't see why I've been left." Listen to what she kept saying: "It isn't *right!*" "*I* don't see why I've been left." It was her thoughts that caused her not to be able to see out of her left eye.

Elizabeth's husband had just passed away, and she was angry. She wasn't feeling grief, she was feeling rejection; and his death was the ultimate rejection. How dare he die!

It wasn't the eye she was even interested in. Fun-loving types don't worry about their illnesses. They can be dying and not be concerned. "Oh, don't worry about it," they'll say. Obviously, her disorder was the response of her subconscious to her rage. Once she had overcome her anger, her sight returned.

THE HEALTHIEST OF THE THREE

As adults, Fun-loving Children will probably remain the truly healthiest of all the three groups. Any health difficulties they do encounter are normally under their own subconscious control, although they are rarely aware of it. They have a subconscious that will not allow itself to be dominated or influenced in its learning years by the expectations and demands of others; indeed, their subconscious quickly learns how to use the situation to control others, whether through, attitude or health.

As with Fun-loving Children in early years, the grown-up Fun-loving Children (the Flamboyant Adults), quickly learn how to have their own way and to gain the attention they crave. These people are too controlling to allow anyone to be responsible for how they live their lives. One of the reasons why people of this personality type usually enjoy remarkably good health is that they rarely reject themselves. With incredible self-confidence, they maintain self-respect despite widespread rejection by others.

As adults, Fun-loving Children find it less easy to throw temper tantrums than they did during earlier years. So, while some continue throwing tantrums throughout their lives, most turn to other means of attracting the attention they need. The subconscious is a vital ally in this campaign. Of the three types, the Fun-loving has the subconscious most talented at mimicry, which is probably why such people make good actors. Their subconscious can mimic anything it chooses to copy, including any health condition. It can copy a disease so perfectly that few health specialists will be able to detect it from the real thing.

This is the group where many miracle healings come from. Rejection characters can just as easily cure themselves as they can make themselves sick.

It would be unkind and untrue to say that an individual is deliberately causing their own illness or that they have logical control over their own recovery. The truth is, the subconscious causes the problem, either to attract attention or to gain some other advantage of control. It is control of their own and other peoples' situations that Fun-loving Children need in order to feel accepted.

If Fun-loving Children can't control you
they feel rejected.

A STUDY IN HEALING: THREE SISTERS

Sandra suffered from a severe case of arthritic hands. Because she lived alone and was unable to do anything for herself, her two sisters would visit her everyday to do her housework. They brought Sandra to see me.

After the first healing, everyone seemed overjoyed. The pain had gone away. But about ten days later, Sandra visited me again, with hands just as gnarled and painful as before. Again the healing treatment was successful, and again the pain went; but this time, the "cure" lasted only five days before she returned to me.

For some reason, the healing was lasting less time after each visit, while normally I would expect the reverse to happen. Casually, I asked Sandra, "What would happen if your sisters didn't visit?"

Before I could finish the sentence, she snapped back, "They have to visit! I can't manage on my own!"

There was the subconscious "reason" for her arthritis. After this discovery, Sandra's sisters promised that they would continue to visit her whether her hands were disabled or not. When she began to trust that her sisters would not abandon her even if she didn't need them to do her chores, the arthritis disappeared.

A TASTE FOR COMPETITION

Fun-loving Children seem to enjoy pressure, they respond to it without ill effect. They're able to strike a balance between life's pleasures and its demands, and they always seem to work within their abilities and enjoy the challenge. In fact, I've yet to find a true Fun-loving type who can be pressured.

Fun-loving Children enjoy working or playing in exacting situations that neither the Serious nor the Passive can tolerate. This ability, of course, puts them in control. To them, havoc means attention; and attention is what they crave. Some will even go so far as to create a sense of urgency where actually there is none called for. These are the children who benefit most from competition, and thus they are the ones who should be sent to competitive schools. In love with attention, they need to pour their natural enthusiasm into physical and mental effort.

If sports are their thing, they will succeed without the physical injuries endured by Serious types. They are too relaxed to get hurt. And while Fun-loving extroverts enjoy competition, they rarely take it so seriously as to stress themselves out. They can accept losing. To the Fun-loving, life is a game to be enjoyed, and not being on top doesn't stop them from putting more effort into what they do. This is the attitude to have if you are going to push yourself hard and avoid stress-related health problems. Of course, if they fail some test or interview, they will be upset. But not for long.

When success comes, it comes naturally; they seem to achieve it without trying. Their ability to stay happy and have fun, even under pressure, is amazing.

The Fun-loving students have mobile minds and can easily stray from one grand idea to another. Therefore, they need more positive guidance than children of the other types. Fun-loving Children need parental direction in their lives, and respond well to parental firmness. In fact, they expect it. Remember, it is attention they crave; and if they feel they are being ignored, they will switch from one ambition or idea to another. Life's actors, their minds are quick and their attitude is, to a degree, irresponsible. They recognize these traits, just as all children basically know their strengths and weaknesses.

Fun-loving Children are not enamored of status, they are not committed to every activity's end result. They just want to be noticed and have fun in whatever they are doing. These happy people like to be admired and noticed; they like to be involved in everything, and at a high-profile level.

Allow them this attention and they will flourish.

__To the Fun-loving, social acceptance__
__is more important than academic acclaim.__

Reminders
Fun-loving Children

Fun-loving children have a fear of rejection.

Fun-loving children take nothing seriously. To them, life is one big game.

Fun-loving children demand activity and attention.

The demands Fun-loving children make upon others are endless.

Children who are boisterous and full of fun feed on other people's energy. They need involvement in your affairs.

Fun-loving children try to control everybody's life.

Fun-loving children have no respect for privacy.

To the emotional child there is no such thing as personal space, they own it all.

The life force of Fun-loving children is attention from others.

These extrovert children do well in high profile situations.

If your child is an extrovert, they will enjoy competitive pressure.

No child likes to feel rejected or unloved.

If Fun-loving children can't control you, they feel rejected.

Fun-loving children can't be pressured. Don't waste your energies trying to change their ways.

Fun-loving children will join gangs or groups if they feel ignored at home.

CHAPTER 4

THE PASSIVE CHILD:
A Fear of Disapproval

NOT A STATUS SYMBOL

For parents who enjoy their children as status symbols, the Passive Child has little to offer. Quiet, submissive, undemanding, this child is constantly trying to please.

The Passive Child lacks the qualities the other two characters use to stand out. Serious Children fulfill their parents' demands for ever-greater success. Fun-loving Children delight at parties, excel at social events, and are beautiful extroverts to show off to friends and family. None of this potential is available to the parent of the Passive Child. This gentle, sensitive being, often full of common sense and more intuition than logic, fears being the center of attention.

More than any of the others, these children want to be helpful, take another's burden to themselves. But because of their size, inexperience or general placid attitude they are often pushed aside. Anything that causes hurt or disturbance in another person's life is something they dread. To them disapproval means they have hurt or rejected someone and an over developed sense of guilt causes them to fear any action or statement signaling disapproval.

Passive Children want nothing more than a smile and a hug, to be accepted as they are. To them, being loved means being able to be a small adult. Needing to be among grown-ups, these boys and girls avoid anything that might cause them selves to be noticed and sent away. And since they fear being a burden, they'll spend their lives trying to help others, rather than expecting help. These youngsters will spend most of their childhood years following their mother or father around, trying to be mature.

These are truly beautiful children. They are mild-mannered, no trouble to friends and family, and have a built-in desire to care for everyone, especially those in need. They appreciate grandparents who have time to sit quietly with them. Passive Children tend to be ignored at times because of the more demanding ways of their Serious or Fun-loving brothers and sisters. Because of their extreme sensitivity, they are easily embarrassed, a condition to which their Fun-loving siblings are quite impervious.

Love to a Passive Child is being asked to help
with the family chores.

THE FAMILY SLAVE

Taking everything literally, Passive Children react badly to teasing. These sensitive youngsters may give the impression of enjoying a joke at their expense; but at a deeper level, they will be hurt and will begin to withdraw from situations involving excitement. They are prone to guilt, at times soaking it up like a sponge. Adults and other children will quickly recognize this tendency; and with careful comments, can make these Passive types do almost anything. The Serious child will bully, and the Fun-loving will cause a scene in order to control. If parents allow this dynamic to go on, the Passive Child can easily wind up as the family slave.

Not all Passive Children submit so weakly to domineering family members. Indeed, some are strong and determined. But even these youngsters will put others before themselves and do almost anything to avoid causing trouble.

Passive Children have little idea about controlling their own lives, and certainly would never think of controlling the lives of others. Thus, they are easily controlled by others who seek to dictate their lives via guilt-inducing comments. Parents must be particularly careful when a Passive Child wants something and ensure that it is really what the *child* wants, not what the child thinks the *parent* wants. Remember, this child's only desire in life is to please and most of the time, Passive types will put others' interests before their own.

Passive Children need their own space, a place they can

call their own, where they can imagine, dream and live out their fantasies without being disturbed. While they are more tolerant than their Serious siblings, and wouldn't complain even if they wanted to, depriving them of a place of their own, or giving them space only to invade it if visitors come to stay, will cause them to retire into themselves. Without a personal, private space in their own home, they will look for such a refuge inside their own thoughts; and their withdrawal is what permits their subconscious to overtake them with doubts and anxieties.

Passive Children have a fear of being a burden

DESTRUCTIVE INSTRUCTIONS

The Passive Child usually prefers solitude or the company of adults to being involved in parties, games and clubs. The greatest joy comes from being asked to help in adult activities. It doesn't matter what's going on, washing the dishes, cleaning the house, looking after someone who is sick, the greatest disappointment is to be overlooked or treated as if incapable.

The Passive Child has a slender hold on self-worth, and it can be lost at a tender age if parents are not aware of their child's needs. Hypersensitive to feelings of guilt, these sensitive boys and girls are prone to emotional blackmail, a means of control often used unknowingly by parents and other caregivers.

When the adolescent needs to leave home, parents often issue forth with comments that imply guilt: "I will miss you,"

"I'm lonely without you," "I worry about you," "You don't phone," or "I was worried." These remarks, and dozens of others, are incredibly effective at keeping the Passive Children under parental control no matter how old they are. I've known parents who deliberately control Passive Children right through life with their guilt-producing comments. These seemingly offhand remarks strike at the heart of sensitive children whose only desire is to help and avoid being a burden.

Throwaway comments may also cause the Passive Children to lose their sense of self-worth and self-respect. "You are always in the way!" can only bring on guilt. A particularly cruel one is, "Now look at what you've made me do!" The child is only trying to help, and it's usually the adult who made the mistake anyway. Most emotionally damaging are comments like, "You will never be any good!" or "You should be ashamed of yourself " Can you imagine what such words do to destroy their recipient's self-esteem? To emotionally sensitive children, such comments are instructions to dislike themselves.

I've treated hundreds of beautiful people who have no self-worth because they were instructed to dislike themselves as children. Perhaps that instruction took the form of a comparison to someone whom the instructor held in low regard. "You're just like your father!" or "You're just like your mother!" a parent might say when feeling annoyed, with no one around to blame but the poor child.

"Don't be stupid!" will cause the child to grow into an adult without a sense of intellectual worth. "Stop crying." "Grow up!" "You're always wanting something." Passive Children take literally your damning comments about their personality. These children need to be told how beautiful they are; they need to be told they are valued and loved, because they often lack the strength to believe it for themselves. Totally trusting, they believe whatever adults say about them. And their trust is too often abused, leaving them to live their lives without the confidence and self-respect necessary to achieve.

> *With no means of defense,*
> *Passive Children are utterly dependent upon parents,*
> *teachers and other caring adults to preserve their*
> *self-worth for them.*

CONSTRUCTIVE ASSIGNMENTS

These children respond to love and encouragement in a quiet, undemanding way. When pressured to do better, however, they only become detached and withdrawn. Due to their immense self-doubt, most of their health problems are emotionally based.

The Passive Child lives on the edge of anxiety. I know this may sound extreme; but the disorders caused by the build-up of insensitive, guilt-laden comments are too numerous to list. Phobias, allergies, multiple sclerosis, depression, rheumatoid arthritis, and many types of cancer are but a few of the forms of body language used by the subconscious on the Passive Child.

It's not always easy to attend to the Passive Child's needs. If you are expecting a houseful of guests in a half-hour and are behind in the preparations, the last thing you need is a six- or seven-year-old trying to help you make the salad. But your comment, "Not now, dear, or I'll be late," will leave your sensitive son or daughter feeling unneeded and unwanted, in the way. Why not ask this eager little helper to go and dust the furniture or straighten the papers? Ask for any help that will give the child a feeling of involvement and importance. To the Passive Child, such assignments are not pressure, but acknowledgment. The Fun-loving Child would see such a request as rejection. But the Passive Child is quite happy to be given tasks, which they perform on their own. Their delight is to be of service; and hence, they derive great pleasure from looking after the elderly. When they are denied the opportunity to do so because they are not fast enough, or for any other valid reason, they feel abandoned and guilty.

Passive Children are the ones most likely to suffer health problems as a result of a parent's lack of understanding. All it takes to set them up for a lifetime of worry or pain is to remove their self-respect and replace it with guilt. Fear of disapproval will do the rest.

A TALENT FOR SELF-REJECTION

We humans are probably the only animals on the planet capable of self-rejection; and among us, the Passive Child is the most capable.

Unlike Fun-loving Children, who recognize rejection at the hands of others but never experience self-rejection, Passive Children are rarely rejected by others but will reject themselves at the slightest cause. Once self-respect and confidence have been removed, the Passive personality rejects itself with thoughts like "I'm not worthy," or "I'm not good enough." And as self-rejection sets in, the subconscious will begin to destroy that part of the anatomy most closely linked to the guilty thought. Cancer, depression, allergies, and many other forms of self-destructive body language are likely to be associated with the Passive Child

Unfortunately girls are more likely to suffer self rejection because they get a double dose of it. They are all too often compared with boys especially if their brothers are one of the other personalities. It is hard to believe that in this so called enlightened age there are still cultures and societies that treat girls and of course women, as if they were in some way inferior. Passive boys in a male aggressive dominated family or society also have their self respect stripped away just because they are different.

A child does not have to do anything, say anything or be anything to be special.
They are special just because they are there.

A DIFFERENT NEED FOR LOVE

Because controlling the subconscious fear of guilt takes an incredible amount of energy, Passive Children will often display much less vitality than either Serious or Fun-loving Children. Not being naturally aggressive they lack the inner drive to argue or fight to preserve their rights or status in the family or classroom. They divert their energies inwards to control submissive fears. When the childhood guilt and fears are released through healing, changes in the temperament of Passive Children can be extraordinary. When they can see themselves for the spiritual beings they are and value themselves for the love they are they can become quite assertive. But always in caring and loving ways, with thoughts focused on the needs of others. Passive Children care very much what people think of them. Their need for love is different from that of Serious and Fun-loving siblings: the Serious Child needs love as approval, and the Fun-loving Child needs love as attention, but the Passive Child needs love as affection. These boys and girls need to be loved as much as they need to love others.

All children and adults need love, approval, and attention. It's the way each child and adult reacts to an abundance or deficiency of love based on any of those three essential human elements that will direct their future character and health.

If there is one thing that should be put above the reach of another human being, it is a child's self respect.

TEACHING THE PASSIVE CHILD

The educational needs of Passive Children have to be carefully considered. Though often highly intelligent and capable of incredible feats, they rarely make full use of their gifts. Tending to be more creative than logical, more artistic than methodical, their sensitive nature will not allow them to push past others. With neither the need to win nor prove something like the Serious child, nor the lust for attention like the Fun-loving Child, the Passive Child prefers to go unnoticed and would rather withdraw from competition than cause another child to feel inadequate.

Passive Children usually give everything of themselves to please others; if ever given reason to believe they have not tried hard enough or have in some way given offense, they are consumed by guilt.

We seem to have lost focus on what schooling is all about. It is not a competition to see who is the best kid on the block. Examinations and grades are not a method of distributing self worth. Our learning years are there to help us find our potential in happiness by guiding us to release natural abilities.

Examinations and test results should not be used to embarrass children or to pressure them by comparison with others. Would you, the parent or teacher like the results of your efforts at work posted up for all to see as a means of applying pressure to you or someone else?

I have always maintained that school reports should be written more with the parent in mind than the child on a basis of how will the parent react towards their child's performance. There are many reasons why a child may not be doing well, or even why they are. Find the cause of success or lack of it as it may not be what is upper most in the student's mind. Pressure from other areas in their life could be causing the problem.

Parents and teachers must take care as they direct and instruct a Passive Child. I have many adults boast of "treating all my children the same," but it isn't something to be proud of. Children are not all alike. They have different needs intellectually, socially, and within the family; and those needs must be satisfied if children are to grow into well-adjusted, healthy adults.

If Passive Children are too forcefully encouraged to be more extroverted, they will only develop anxiety and the feeling that they are not good enough.

Fun-loving Children want to be openly appreciated; and without clearly demonstrated attention to their efforts, they feel rejected. Serious Children need private, but positive, approval; and they need to hear comments like, "Well done," and "You're trying hard." Passive Children need only understanding and gentle love shown through kind words.

The worst thing parents or teachers can do to adversely affect the future health of any child is to publicly belittle them. Fun-loving characters will quickly get over it, but drawing attention to the inadequacies of Passive or Serious Children will rob them of their self-respect.

> *Once self-respect is lost the Passive Child is unlikely to regain it, without a good deal of help.*

Passive Children do not like the eyes of the world upon them. Easily embarrassed, these sensitive youngsters will quit trying if parents give their skills high-profile treatment. Neither should teachers overindulge Passive Children with accolades, because they will underachieve to avoid recognition. Kind encouragement and praise are all that's needed. Passive Children will achieve to please others; Fun-loving Children will achieve for attention; and Serious Children will achieve to prove themselves to others.

> *A smile of appreciation and a whispered 'Thank you' is all it takes to maintain a Passive Child's self respect.*

SCHOOLING

Deciding which school you send your Passive Child to is crucial. If your Passive Child is a high achiever a high-powered school that demands excellence may be an excellent choice provided it is their choice and they are not made to feel pressured because of your expectations. However if your child is excessively passive and non competitive a high powered school is not the best choice. If they believe in any way that they are not achieving to the school's standards or yours, they'll be full of guilt. The subsequent loss of self-worth will affect their development. These Passive boys and girls are disposed to be critical of themselves and their efforts so they must not be expected to perform in a demanding academic arena, with over-bearing parents only augmenting their low self-image. The Passive Child often does better when attending a less prominent school, an institution with an atmosphere which is more artistic and less competitive, one that blends with the child's creative nature.

If Passive Children are to become happy, guilt-free, healthy adults, avoid any situation in which they are singled out from the crowd. They are private people who prefer to work quietly, they are more likely to hide their success than risk being the center of attention.

Quiet understanding and acknowledgment of the love they are,
is all Passive Children ask for.
These are probably the most undemanding of all children.

A STUDY IN HEALING: ONE LIFE'S GUILTY BEGINNING

A Passive Child who is made to feel guilty, for any reason, will turn the hurt inward, beginning on a path of self-destruction leading to a multitude of emotional problems.

A typical example was Alan, a clever, sensitive man, who, although constantly trying to please, always felt he was of no value and not really liked. All his life, he'd considered himself a burden to his family, friends, and employers, changing his job several times because he thought he just wasn't good enough. His self-worth was practically nil.

The reason quickly became apparent when I helped him regress to the time of his birth. Alan recalled his parents worry at wondering how they were going to be able to pay for this fourth child's education, clothes and other expenses that would have to be added to the financial burden that they already had. Listening to his parents worrying about the hardship of caring for the new addition, Alan was consumed with guilt. And as an adult, his subconscious remembered the reaction at his birth, he was overwhelmed with a sense of responsibility for the problems he had created just by being born, even though at a logical level he couldn't remember the incidents.

This extreme assumption of guilt is typical of this personality. Passive Children feel guilty even when the fault isn't theirs.

Alan began life feeling guilty, and it got worse as he grew. Whenever his parents complained of being tired, overworked, or short of money, Alan's very overdeveloped sense of responsibility would make him feel worthless and in the way. He thought of himself as the cause of his parents' troubles. These feelings followed him into his adult life. During healing, I was able to show how, if he were in his parents' shoes, he would have felt just as burdened as they had, but would certainly not have expected the baby to assume any blame or have been loved less because of it.

Explaining the other point of view is the best way of reversing feelings of guilt. It shows just how careful parents must be if they have sensitive, Passive Children.

> *Guilt hangs around the lives of Passive Children*
> *like an albatross waiting to force them down.*

Reminders
Passive Children

Passive children have a fear of disapproval.

The Passive child does not like public attention.

Love to the Passive child is being asked to help with family chores.

Passive children need to be hugged or held.

This sensitive youngster reacts badly to teasing.

Passive children have a fear of being a burden.

These children are easily embarrassed.

Passive children can too easily end up being the family slave.

Be sure that when this child wants something it is really what they want and not what they believe the parent wants.

A quiet space of their own is essential to the Passive child.

With no means of defense, Passive children are utterly dependent upon parents, teachers and other caring adults to preserve their self-worth for them.

When pressured these children become detached and withdrawn.

Passive children are plagued with immense self doubt.

If denied the opportunity to be of service, they feel abandoned and guilty.

Passive children are experts at self-rejection. Your disapproval of some part of their lives or activity will often rob them of their self-respect.

If you give the Passive child reason to believe they have offended, they are consumed by guilt.

Examinations are not a method of distributing self-worth.

A school report is more a family report than a child's report. It is an indication of a child's intents and fears more than ability.

Passive children develop anxiety if pressured.

Ambition is not usually high in this child's mind, preferring to be a servant rather than a leader.

These are probably the most undemanding of all children.

Guilt hangs around the lives of Passive children like an albatross waiting to force them down.

Chapter 5

LOVING YOUR CHILDREN

ONLY ONE WAY

There is only one-way to love anyone: unconditionally, with nothing whatsoever required in exchange for that love. We either accept or love someone totally, or we reject them. We can't reject this part but accept that part. Children know who love them, who accept them, just as they are.

Parental love is the strongest love of all. Of course, unconditional love in no way precludes parents' disciplining their young ones. Guidance and discipline, lovingly applied, improve a child's character and give the tools needed to grow up to be a happy, healthy adult. When parents love their child absolutely, with no reservation, they will do all they can to ensure every opportunity life can offer.

Children should not have to do anything to feel accepted and loved.

A parent's love should be unlimited, unqualified, unrestricted.

EMPTY POCKETS, BUT A FULL HEART

I know a woman who has a most difficult life. She has no husband, a child with terrible deformities, and no source of income except that which the government provides. This woman is shunned by most people because she sometimes smokes, uses abusive language, and, once a week, while a friend looks after her pitiful child, goes out for a drink. People avoid her because they feel she is socially unacceptable. But to me, she is an angel.

I know of no other living person who would love her poor, deformed, little girl as unconditionally she does. Her love pours out for her child, and she has given everything she possesses to ensure that the child is loved and knows she is loved. So much love pours out of this woman that other children in need of love are drawn to her. You can see the love shine bright in their eyes for this woman who has nothing and does nothing except "love." Many people avoid or criticize her; but to me, she stands head and shoulders above them all, a beacon of love in an often loveless society.

Children don't value us for what we give them,
but for the love we are for them.

AN UNFAIR CHOICE

Children need to know that both parents love them unconditionally. Of course this applies only when the child knows both parents. More importantly, they need to be able to express their love for both parents without feeling that they must choose between one and the other. When a mother says, "Wait till your father gets home," she is telling her child, "Your father doesn't love or understand you as much as I do." To a child, that hurts.

When a mother or father use the other parent to threaten, the Serious Child takes it as pressure to please the parent making the statement. But he or she will also lose respect for the adult applying the threat, in the above case, the mother. They will not admire the father any less, for Dad has the strength they want to emulate. By shifting the blame, the mother will cast herself as weak and trying to come between the child and the father.

The Fun-loving Child will take the same remark to signify rejection by the mother and acceptance by the father. This child hears: "Wait till your father gets home" as "I'm not interested in what you do; I'll just dump it all in your father's lap." The Fun-loving Child wants attention, and wants it now. She or he is not notably naughty but can't wait until father arrives to be noticed and will respond to any postponement of attention by becoming even more demanding. Eventually, this little scamp will become enough of a nuisance to be punished, a fate, oddly enough, that may well be preferred to being ignored.

The Passive Child rarely draws threats, but when it happens, it's probably because this little adult is trying to help out with some chore or errand. Comments like "Don't bother me now," or "If you do that again, I'll tell your father," erode self-respect. Afraid of causing trouble or being a burden, a Passive Child will stop communicating. (Of course, for all three groups of children, the situation would be exactly the same were it the father leaving the responsibility for discipline to his wife.)

Children love both parents; their respect and love for any parent will shrink if that parent tries to steer the child's love from the other partner to himself or herself. If you have become a one parent family because of separation or divorce about the worst thing you can do to your child is complain about the other parent.

Children love and want to be loved by both parents.

If someone at school makes fun of their parents they know how to respond, though children rarely make fun of other children's parents. These are boundaries they rarely cross.

Children do not like to hear their parent criticized; but when it's one of the parents doing it, they become confused, hurt, and withdrawn. They don't know how to react. If forced to make a choice between one parent or the other, they will love the one they're being asked to turn away from though it's unlikely you will realize it at the time. The parent they remain with is their security and they are not in a position to threaten that security but let there be no doubt in your mind, one day they will hold the parent who forced them to take sides, fully responsible.

Of course if the situation which caused the family separation is because of some form of abuse, the children will be more understanding of the complaining parent, but that doesn't mean that they like to hear it.

> *It is emotional abuse to use children to vent your anger*
> *against those they love.*
> *If you do you will lose their love and respect.*

AN ILLOGICAL EMOTION

Loving children of the three personalities in the unique manner each requires is one of the joys of raising children.

Loving Serious Children unconditionally means letting them know that your loving support is not conditioned on their success. If a parent withdraws love and attention over a low grade, or shows displeasure over a poor effort, Serious Children will begin to overexert themselves. They will exceed healthy stress levels while laboring to win back the favors and the acclaim they feel they've lost.

The ability to demonstrate love will be almost nonexistent in the Assertive Adult who was unloved as a Serious Child. Serious Children need to be taught, through example, how to express emotions; if not, they will be unable to react to love once they've matured, and will give the impression that love is something weak and unimportant. It will be just one more rung on the ladder of failure or success; and with their deeply ingrained fear of failure, they'll probably avoid getting involved at all. Emotion cannot be logically explained; thus, they avoid it.

Love should never be withheld as a form of discipline.
The phrase 'If you do that I won't love you' is obscene.

THE SQUEAKY WHEEL GETS THE OIL.

Giving unconditional love to Fun-loving Children may sound easy enough; but, however much you give, it will never be enough, for they will be demanding of your love and attention all the time. If a child of this personality thinks you are paying more attention to a sibling, he or she will do something, anything, to attract the focus back to self. Yet, if this active little boy or girl knows your love and attention are centered on them, they'll give the impression of being uninterested in you while trying to secure the same notice from others.

Fun-loving Children, both during childhood and as adults, need love that is active. Their need is not for the encouraging love required by Serious Children and adults. They have enough of that for themselves. Nor must they have the quiet love needed by Passive Children and adults. The Fun-loving type want love to revolve around conversation and activity.

Fun-loving people are demonstrative; to them love is a "doing thing," an unending involvement in your affairs. Fun-loving Children who have been deprived of love come to fear rejection. To protect themselves, he or she never allows their love to become too involved or too deep, pulling back every time true intimacy is approached. With little emotional investment in a relationship, they can bounce back quickly from rejection.

70

Most Fun-loving Children think they have been hurt too often to trust their own emotions. Nevertheless, these people go out of their way to prove the opposite. They go from person to person, relationship to relationship, performing great displays of affection and uttering promises of undying love; but rarely can they give of themselves totally. When they do, their love and attention for one person is absolute. However, if they believe that their love has been rejected, they will explode in rage and anger as all previous rejection comes rushing out in one moment of life.

When a Fun-loving type has a history of rejection, she or he rarely can satisfy either self or another for very long; but if loved as a child, their adult love will be intense and long-lived.

SEEN BUT NOT HEARD.
Passive Children, the quietest of the three personalities are the easiest to overlook. Although they need affection just as powerfully as anyone else, these children will rarely make a fuss if they're forgotten, blaming themselves instead of their parents. Having a Fun-loving sibling is particularly difficult for them. In the midst of the Fun-loving Child's hubbub, the Passive Child can easily be lost. And if ignored intentionally, Passive Children will feel hurt and sad but will not respond in any way except to draw deeper into themselves. If they are shown unconditional love that allows them to participate as a helper and not a leader, however, they'll excel. These children, so often overlooked, are the most

generous and unconditional in the giving of their own love.

Adult Passive Children are deeply wounded when their love is rejected. But they will not waste the love that is spurned, it will be added to the love they have for the next person they meet. Passive Adults never cease to trust, always believing to have found Mr. or Ms. Right. They have deep needs to love and care for others. While probably most content when they have met and fallen in love with another Passive soul, people of this personality usually give themselves to Serious types because they secretly admire their positive attitudes. A Serious Adult probably won't satisfy a Passive personality's need for love; nonetheless, Passive types will allow their caring and loving abilities full expression.

If you have a Serious Child, teach him or her by example how to express emotion, especially love. If your child is Fun-loving, you must show your love through endless games and activities. And if your child is Passive, be prepared to be loved in a caring and gentle fashion that needs to be returned with only a simple smile and hug of appreciation.

All children are precious.
Love them their way.

Mud Pies

You have had a hard day cleaning the house in expectation of the in-laws who are coming later in the evening. Your little boy is playing in the yard with his friends. Then, before you can stop them he comes into the kitchen covered in mud followed by his friends. They look like a dump truck looking for somewhere to off load a collection of dirt and mud. They find just the place, your nice clean kitchen floor.

Your first reaction is to scream, 'get out of here, look what you have done to my floor.' Confused looks cross four little faces, your child looks hurt and they all withdraw to unload another parcel of mud at your neighbor's house.

That wasn't good tactics. They have learned nothing except your child has an unreasonable mother who understands nothing, they won't go there again, and you are left with the floor to clean.

Next time try this idea. You have four grubby, mud soaked children standing on your nice clean floor. Keep your cool. They love you which is why you've been favored with their mud. Help them off with their clothes, set them around the table and give them cookies and a drink. When they are fully relaxed, off guard thinking what a wonderful mother you are, you drop your little surprise.

"OK, you guys, it's your mud, you clean it up and I want it done in the next hour."

Give them the tools to clean up and a lovely big smile. When they leave an hour later they will still love you but will leave the mud outside the next time.

Children who are made to feel responsible
for what they do at an early age,
learn to respect other peoples situations.

Reminders
Loving Your Children

There is only one way to love anybody; unconditionally.

Children should not have to do anything to feel accepted and loved.

A parent's love should be unlimited, unqualified and unrestricted.

Children don't value us for what we give them but for the love we are for them.

Children need to know that both parents love them unconditionally.

Children need to be free to express their love for both parents.

If afraid of causing trouble, the passive child will stop communicating.

Never make promises you cannot keep.
> Serious children will grow to distrust you.
> Fun-loving children will use it against you.
> Passive children will think you don't love them.

Children love and want to be loved by both parents.

Children do not like to hear parents criticize each other or be expected to take sides.

It is emotional abuse to use children to vent your anger against those they love. If you do you will lose their love and respect.

Children need to know your love is not conditional upon their success.

Love should never be withheld as a form of discipline. The phrase 'If you do that I won't love you' is obscene.

A child does not have to do anything, say anything or be anything to be special. They are special just because they are there.

All children are precious. Love them their way.

Children who are made to feel responsible for what they do at an early age, learn to respect other people's situations.

Chapter 6

SUGGESTIBILITY
The Need to Be Positive

LITTLE, LITERAL MINDS

When we are born, the logical part of the brain isn't very well developed. So the subconscious, the instinctive mind, is what governs the thoughts and actions of the child. It's not until around age ten or eleven for girls and a year or two later for boys that the logical consciousness has both the store of information and the physical capability to take over responsibility for our well-being. Children may appear to be acting logically. They may laugh and seem to joke, but, because their subconscious is in the ascendant, they are highly prone to suggestion, the barrier against it that the logical consciousness will in later years present has not yet been erected.

Remember, children don't joke.
They take everything seriously.

POSITIVE ATTITUDES, NEGATIVE STATEMENTS

One of the most confusing statements a child has to deal with is the '*do not*', where the positive do is followed by the negative not. The child hasn't learned to understand the intricacies of language, and, anyway, the subconscious at the very young age recognizes only positive actions and words. Therefore, when faced with an instruction such as "Do not touch the cat," the child will ignore the negative "not" and act on the positive "do", which means go ahead and touch the cat. You, the parent are now annoyed that the child has apparently deliberately disobeyed. So you repeat the instruction, "I told you not to do that". The child still instinctively ignores the negative "not", repeats what its already been told "not" to do. You are now exasperated and the child is in big trouble. This is why babies do exactly the opposite of what you want when you tell them *not* to do something.

Children are born with solidly positive attitudes; were they born with negative attitudes, they wouldn't survive for long. But adults unknowingly set out to reverse those natural attitudes and to transform children into negative people. Every time a child is disobedient and does the opposite of what you ask, it is because they are instinctively reacting to the positive in your sentence. They just don't hear the word not.

Children do not deliberately want to annoy.
They misunderstand the meaning in your words in the
same way that you don't always understand them.

Serious Children are not so easily trained out of their positive attitudes. Because of their drive to succeed, these boys and girls avoid negative situations which they have learned get them into trouble and act only on positive ones. This training is one of the many reasons why Serious Children become such successful adults. Their outlook is pointedly positive; and in both personal and professional lives, they instinctively steer clear of the negative and only act when there is no negative in the situation.

I recall one little boy who was told not to put his hand on a hot stove. He immediately and before anyone could stop him, put his hand onto the hot stove severely burning his hand. When asked why he had done that he cried through his pain, "You told me to, you told me to" and nothing will convince him, even to this day, that he had been told "*not*" to. His mind had completely blocked out the negative *'not'*.

**Serious children learn quickly that negative
situations are best avoided.**

The Fun-loving Child will also respond to a *'do not'* situation as an invitation to *'do'*. For example, if you say to a young Fun-loving type, "You can 'not' have it", they will expect to have it, not having heard the negative in the statement and in their typical exhibitionist style will go into a temper tantrum at what they see as your actions being different to your words. When scolded for disobedience, these youngsters will react negatively at a subconscious level; that negative energy is what will later surface in the form of physical symptoms or psychosomatic disorders.

Being emotional personalities, Fun-loving Children take a negative instruction as a rejection. They look for and only act on positive statements. But while their logical awareness totally ignores the *not,* their subconscious reacts to the negative for them by converting it into body language, including symptoms of physical disorder that may not emerge until years later. As adults, the Fun-loving personalities are walking contradictions: they give every indication of being positive in what they say and do, but their body language can be entirely negative.

Most children are not naturally naughty. However, babies will eventually come to realize that they should be concentrating on the negative aspects of your conversation. As they listen for the negative *not* in preference to the positive do, the negative attitude is born. Passive Children are most affected by negative phrases, with their guilt-laden emotions. Wanting to please, they quickly overcome their instinctive positive reaction to life and become a negative personality, in order to please the adults around them. This causes them endless emotional health problems later in life.

Passive children reflect the parent's negative attitude.

If you want to keep the Passive Child as a positive personality, the Serious Child as a participating member of the family, and avoid all sorts of physical and emotional problems for the Fun-loving Child, do all you can to avoid the word *not*. Instead of "Do not touch the cat," say "Leave the cat alone." You will be amazed at how your children disobey the first and obey the second. Practice using alternatives to the word not: instead of "Do not talk to strangers," say, "Stay away from strangers"; replace "Do not take drugs" with "Avoid drugs."

By telling children "not" to smoke or "not" to take drugs we may be enforcing an attitude to do the opposite of what we intend at a deeper emotional level. To let them see the harm that drugs and smoking can do is more likely to have an affect than telling them "not" to take drugs. Of course, the real work in producing positive attitudes must be done when children are still in their earliest years when they are unlikely to be offered drugs or even play with matches. Up to the age of ten to thirteen, they will be susceptible to any negatives in your conversation.

Developing a positive attitude in your conversation will reap untold benefits for your children as they make their way to adulthood.

A FAITHFUL DEFENDER

It is only as children change from subconscious control to a degree of independent logical control around the age of puberty that they begin to determine for themselves what represents danger.

Before that time, however, the subconscious is in complete

command of the child's health and safety. A child may appear to be playing happily, but don't doubt for an instant that the sub-conscious defense mechanism is taking note of every situation, faithfully recording in the archives of the memory anything it believes to be harmful to the child's well-being.

I have met with children and adults who suffer nightmares so disturbing that they fear falling asleep. Dreams of being chased by bears, falling off a cliff, or being menaced by ghosts and goblins, the list is endless.

Often these nightmares are caused by no more than a playful adult chasing a terrified child with a soft toy. I remember one teenager who used to wake frequently from a dream of being eaten by a tiger. She described the beast's big red eyes and white teeth; and as it moved closer and closer she began to panic, which woke her from sleep.

It all went back to an uncle who used to think it was great fun to see his little niece making faces and trying to hide under the bed sheets as he came closer and closer to her with a stuffed toy tiger, saying repeatedly, "It's gonna eat you up!" What in heaven's name do adults, even caring ones, think they are doing by such jokes? What is so funny about seeing a young child terrified? And don't be fooled if a Fun-loving Child gives the impression of enjoying such a game; all the while she or he would be just as terrified as other children.

Another client of mine used to wake up in a sweat, gasping for breath, with visions of being suffocated. During treatment we found out that it dated back to being held under the sheets by his older brother when he was a child. His reaction to his brother's bullying was typical of the Passive Child. This type frightens more easily and visibly, compared to the others.

A little girl was brought to me because she would wake up screaming from a recurrent nightmare she had about falling into a pit filled with water. Her terror was the fault of her father, who on just one occasion teased his daughter by holding her over a well and playfully pretending to drop her. Oh, how this innocent little girl remembered the adults laughing as she screamed in terror! Then they became annoyed with the little girl because she didn't laugh; her tears spoiled their fun.

As a result of the incident, the girl later developed a phobia about pools of water. Worse than that, she developed a guilt complex whose origin she could not identify. She came to dislike parties and family gatherings all because of the day when she spoiled everybody's enjoyment and was scolded for being silly. I doubt if her father, who had such a wonderful time teasing her, even remembers the incident that almost ruined her life.

Children do not like to be teased.
It destroys their self-worth, their confidence
and their trust in people.

OUR INTERNAL VCR

These cases are straightforward and once the cause is understood, the problem comes quickly to the surface. But there are other, more subtle ways of programming a child's attitudes. For example, when the television or radio is on and the child appears to be asleep, the subconscious is fully aware of everything that takes place during the film or story; the child's memory will record it all precisely. It's just like playing subliminal tapes while someone's asleep. It's an excellent way to program the subconscious, for the subconscious never sleeps. Imagine a child half-asleep in a room with the TV on and tuned to a vicious adventure movie. Such a film always features stereotypes: the GOOD, the BAD. Although the child is sleeping, the subconscious is on full alert, soaking up every sentence. It documents all the activity and quickly identifies with either the aggressor or the victim.

What choice an individual subconscious makes depends on the personality of the child. The gentle, sensitive child will usually identify with the victim. The more aggressive, serious, attention-seeking child will identify with the aggressor.

No act, no word, will be missed; and at some time later in the child's life, when facing danger reminiscent of the movie, the subconscious will react in a defense mode based on its interpretation of the film, which by then has been long forgotten, that is, by the logical awareness. The person's fear or hostility arises as a direct result of a film the child was *not even watching*, but which was nevertheless engraved onto the subconscious mind.

Exactly the same will happen if children see or hear their parents arguing or, worse, fighting. Don't think that just because your children are asleep or inattentive that they are unaware; their subconscious is filing away every word, action, and emotion for future reference.

Anger is noted by Serious Children, who have to be taught emotion, they will copy it for their own defenses, growing up to use the emotion of anger or violence as a weapon as they seek to protect themselves from the domination of others.

Fun-loving Children will learn how to use the anger they have witnessed to manipulate and control others..

Passive Children are deeply wounded by violent situations. It builds fear and anxiety in their lives.

*Your children's subconscious never sleeps
and will one day repeat in health or emotional activity
what you allowed them to witness.*

A STUDY IN HEALING: A CRIPPLING YARDSTICK

David, now in his late fifties, had been a success by anybody's standards. Even though he'd held several important managerial positions, a feeling that he had not achieved anything with his life plagued him. That he wasn't "good enough." He was sure that he hadn't accomplished what was expected of him.

Healing released the cause of his problem in a single

session. David was able to recall how his father constantly told him as a boy that he didn't "measure up." His father used his son as an excuse to release his own anger. David's subconscious recorded his father's anger, as well as his physical violence; and when an adult and David was faced with something he didn't like, he would unaccountably lash out at members of his own family.

A STUDY IN HEALING: FEAR ON THE STREETS

Peter phoned. Would I see him, he wanted to know. He was desperate. I have noticed that Serious types are prone to phobias; and Peter, a Serious type, exhibited all the symptoms of being in the grip of a phobia.

It had all started one day five years earlier when he was walking along a road. Suddenly, without reason, his whole body froze. Utterly incapable of taking another step forward, he stood there paralyzed for several minutes, until finally he was able to move again. Shortly afterward, he had been hurrying along a street when again, his whole system just stopped. This time, his momentum caused him to fall forward, landing on his face. He also began to notice other abnormalities creeping up on him: for example, a fear of people approaching from the other direction as he walked along a street or corridor. Alarmingly, these symptoms began to occur more regularly.

Peter's condition had been explained as "dead-man's syndrome," about which little was known. It was thought to be some form of neurological disorder. To me, however, it sounded like body language, a case of the subconscious, for some as yet undiscovered reason, suddenly deciding that there was a risk in moving forward. One telling clue was the fear Peter had developed of crossing the road, a fear, he reasoned, due to thinking he might suddenly be unable to move in the middle of traffic.

The reason for his condition quickly surfaced during our session; and it was not an uncommon one, though I must admit that in Peter's case the subconscious reaction had been extreme. Peter began to remember that between the ages of four and six he used to go for walks with his father, often along busy streets. Peter, like a lot of little boys, had a habit of walking along the edge of the sidewalk and sometimes skipping into the road as he did so. And his father, like a lot of fathers, was always telling him, "Stay in the middle of the sidewalk, it's safer!" On one of these outings, Peter stepped off the curb and into the road just as a speeding car passed by, almost knocking him over. Startled by the car, Peter jumped back onto the sidewalk where his father, also in shock, shouted at him. He warned the lad that if he did it again he might be killed; he must stay in the middle of the sidewalk and not cross the road without him. After that, Peter always walked well away from the curb.

In this story we have both elements, fear and guilt, that are necessary to create the subconscious programming of a future phobia. But what, after all these years had triggered the phobia of walking along the street to appear? Why had he suddenly stopped? Why now? The reason for stopping was simple. If the sidewalk was crowded, Peter might be forced to the roadside edge. To prevent this, his subconscious immobilized him until the sidewalk had cleared and the danger had passed. And his subconscious prevented him from crossing the road because his father would not let his young son cross unless he had his hand on an adult's arm.

But these origins of Peter's condition still didn't explain why the phobia hadn't started until he'd reached his forties.

"When did your father die?" I asked.

"About five and a half years ago," he responded.

"Six months before the problem started?"

That was it! We now had the complete picture. When Peter's father died, his subconscious recalled what Peter had been told the day he'd almost been run over so many years ago: "Don't step off the sidewalk or cross the road unless I'm with you," his dad had ordered. Peter's subconscious interpreted the death of Peter's father literally in light of the command it had registered: the father was no longer "with" the son. Peter's subconscious was keeping Peter out of the street and away from the curb because it would not allow the boy to disobey his father.

Your subconscious is always a child.

FOUR CRUCIAL WORDS

By telling the story of Peter, I am not for a minute suggesting that parents not educate and discipline their children on road safety. But when they make statements like "Never cross the road without me," or "Never go outside the yard without me," parents need to add one more little sentence: "Until you're grown up."

I have had clients who became afraid to go outside their own gate, to make friends or speak to strangers. Their condition resulted because when they were little their mother or father, while cautioning them not to go out without them or not to talk to strangers, did not add those final four words, "Until you're grown up." Because of this tiny but crucial omission, many children are "deactivated" in certain situations when the loving parent dies. This problem is likely to increase in the near future as our concern for the safety and well-being of our children escalates in this hostile and dangerous world.

Without the four critical words "Until you're grown up,"
parents risk burdening children with fears and phobias
once those parents have died and left them.

A STUDY IN HEALING: SUCCESSFUL, BUT INDECISIVE

A similar case was that of a successful man who suddenly realized that he was no longer able to make decisions, to do what he needed to do to improve his life.

During his healing session, we discovered that the

paralysis went back to a father who repeatedly told him, "Don't do anything without checking with me first." As he grew older, he always, without realizing it, discussed everything with his father before taking action. His father never interfered or offered advice, he just listened while his son told him what he was about to do. So when his father died, the man was unable to compete with the subconscious program: "Don't do anything without checking with me first." The father had unknowingly programmed his son to stop making decisions when he was no longer there.

Reminders
Suggestibility

Children don't joke; they take everything seriously.

Children do not deliberately want to annoy. They misunderstand the meaning in your words in the same way you don't always understand them.

Young children are confused by the statement, 'do not.' Should they act on the 'do' or on the 'not'?

Serious children learn quickly that negative situations are best avoided.

Passive children reflect the parent's negative attitude.

Children up to the age of 10-12 are susceptible to negatives in your conversation.

Develop a positive attitude in your conversations, you and your children will benefit.

A child's mind never sleeps and it listens to what the child is inattentive to.

Never put fear into a child's mind if it can be avoided. The fear develops in the mind proportionately to the child's years.

Teasing which is fun to you can cause abject fear in the mind of the child.

Your few minutes of fun at a child's expense may cost the child years of humiliating fear as a phobia.

Teasing destroys a child's self worth, their confidence and their trust in people.

It is not what children actively see that controls their later reaction, but what they subconsciously interpret.

Your child's subconscious never sleeps and will one day repeat in health or emotional activity what you allowed them to witness.

Serious children copy anger and violence for protection. Fun-loving children use anger and violence to control. Passive children fear violence and anger and become defensive and anxious.

When instructing your child on safety and security, always add the words, 'until you are an adult.'

Whatever is said to someone who is in shock will become a reality.

The power of the subconscious to control the logical mind is incredible.

CHAPTER 7

ALLERGIES AND PHOBIAS:
A Surprising Similarity

In truth, there is little difference between an allergy and a phobia. Both usually arise as a result of childhood trauma, and are treated by breaking the link between the present condition and the deep-seated cause. Fear, compounded by guilt, is the basis of all phobias and of many allergies, which, not infrequently, are no more than inverted phobias. Passive types, therefore, so often racked by guilt, are most susceptible to such disorders.

I think I should add here that occasionally allergies and phobias have a cause that goes back to beyond birth and there is little prevention the parent can do when the child's subconscious brings into this life something that happened in another life.

A MILKY MESSAGE

Doesn't it seem strange to you that a high proportion of allergies involve milk? When doctors diagnose patients as "lactose intolerant," they tell them to give up milk; and, in most instances, the allergy goes away if the patient follows the advice.

But only occasionally, when cow's milk is introduced to the child too early in life is drinking milk really the cause of the patient's discomfort. The reaction to milk is a symptom, not a cause. Once again, we're dealing with body language.

A STUDY IN HEALING: ON THE (MILK) WAGON

Suddenly, and for no apparent reason, Ben had become allergic to milk. He first noticed something was wrong when the condition of his skin mysteriously changed. He had always been healthy. Now in his late fifties, however, his skin had become tender, and his energy level had dropped. He felt chronically drained and "out of it." He hadn't a clue as to what was causing him this distress.

As the months progressed, he began to lose weight, falling from a healthy 180 pounds down to a skinny 145. His doctors had given him every test imaginable: no blood problem; all functions working perfectly; and scans and x-rays were clear. He had tried several types of drugs and homeopathic remedies, all to no avail. In miserable condition, he took a friend's suggestion and visited a dietitian, who, diagnosing his problem as an allergy to milk, put him on a diary-free eating plan. Over the next few months, Ben's health improved dramatically. He assumed that all he had to do was stay away from milk and his problems would be over. Have you ever tried to live on a diet totally free of milk? It is virtually impossible. Almost every meal placed in front of us has milk or milk by-products in it somewhere. Eating out or going to parties became difficult for Ben. He noticed that if he was served any food which had been mixed with or contained any derivative of milk he would become ill within a few hours.

Ben explained that he had first noticed the allergy about four years earlier. When I inquired what trauma had taken place in his life six to nine months prior to that, he told me his wife had left him. With that information, we delved into his subconscious. A memory soon surfaced of his parents fighting and arguing over father's drinking habits. Ben at the time was just a few months old and still bottle feeding.

His father's drinking problem worsened over time, to the point that Ben's mother was constantly warning him that unless he kept off the bottle she would leave him. She made good on her threat when Ben was still very young, walking out on her husband and taking Ben with her. Ben recalled her telling family and friends that it was his father's own fault. "He should have given up the bottle when I told him to!" Ben's mother proclaimed.

Now stop here just for a moment. Can you imagine what was going through little Ben's subconscious mind? Mother left Father because Father hadn't "given up the bottle." But the only bottle Ben was aware of was his baby bottle. To little Ben, therefore, his mother's account of the breakup meant if mother ever threatened to leave him he must give up his bottle, his MILK bottle! The point was not forgotten by Ben's subconscious memory; and when, years later, his wife left him, he was devastated, and desperately wanted her back. So his subconscious sprang into action, instructing him: "Give up the (milk) bottle, and she will return." Thus was Ben's allergy to milk born. Ben's phobia to milk was made worse because he was a Passive type who was prone to guilt. He held himself responsible for his wife's departure and desperately wanted to please. He would do what-ever was necessary to persuade his wife to return. On deeper investigation, it also became apparent that he suffered from a guilt complex regarding his father, and this emotion had some-thing to do with Ben's not giving up his bottle when his father was told to leave.

> *Most of us can drink milk without any ill effects.*
> *If you have an allergic reaction to milk,*
> *Ask your subconscious what it is trying to tell you.*

FOOD, FEAR, PROGRAMMING

I believe that the majority of allergies spring from child-hood trauma. The problem is not the food or drink. It is some long-forgotten fear. The allergy is just a symptom of that fear, and the taste or smell of the food was on the mind at the fear's origin. Sometimes allergies result from children being forced to eat something they don't like at the same time that they are undergoing a high level of stress. The association between the food and the trauma is noted at the subconscious level, and if the child faces a similar threat in adult years, the subconscious responds with body language, an allergy intended to warn the adult of the impending danger. Hence, the association develops between a particular food and a particular trauma.

Allergies also arise because of something eaten that was not fresh or was contaminated. The food poisoning is logged by the subconscious, which, considering the offending food forever dangerous, institutes an allergic reaction as a warning the next time you go to eat it.

Obesity, too, can be rooted deep in the subconscious, which never stops acting to fulfill the needs it identified during a person's early years. If Fun-loving Children, deprived of what they consider sufficient attention, are told repeatedly by parents and family members what a good boy or girl they are for finishing every bite of their dinner, the subconscious programs eating into its memory as essential for attention. The adult's subconscious urge to eat in situations of loneliness or neglect is then too strong to resist.

Phobias and allergies are classic examples of what the subconscious can do to prevent you from doing a second time something that caused you great anxiety the first time. They are based on fears and guilt that you cannot remember, but that still persist to bring fear whenever a similar situation presents itself.

LOADING THE GUN, PULLING THE TRIGGER

Most young girls are extremely sensitive when it comes to their figure. Think of the guilt instilled in an impressionable preteen by a throwaway remark like, "You look like you're getting fat. You should do something about it." Even if the youngster isn't fat at all, such a comment can easily make her phobic over her weight. Anorexia often results in this way, although the phobic response may not occur until later in life when it is triggered by a similar remark.

The first careless remark usually loads the emotional gun, creating an internal emotion that cements the fear. And the second incident pulls the trigger, bringing about a reaction to the earlier statement. This sequence is why people often believe they know the cause of their phobia: they believe the condition to have resulted from the more recent event. Yet the symptoms persist if that's the explanation they accept. They remember only the trigger. It's the earlier incident, which they don't recall, that caused the problem. Only by bringing that original situation to logical awareness will the link between past and present be achieved and the phobia ended.

A STUDY IN HEALING: A BELLYFUL OF SODA

Twenty-eight-year-old Fiona, anorexic since she was seventeen, rarely weighed above sixty-five pounds. Since the onset of her condition, she'd spent most of her time in and out of clinics, receiving various forms of psychiatric and psychological therapy, all to no avail. Now she was afflicted with a severe kidney disorder, had lost most of her teeth, and suffered many other damaging problems because of her eating disorder. I was told she was anorexic due to a deep desire for attention, which came from being the youngest of several children. I judged Fiona to be Passive and prone to guilt, not the sort who would seek to attract attention to herself.

I have always believed, and have never been given any cause to change my belief, that anorexia and bulimia are no more than phobias. Fiona's problem was no different.

Healing quickly revealed the disorder's cause. As a three-year-old, she drank a lot of soda at a party, causing her belly to swell and hurt. Friends and family made fun of how she looked and felt, telling her she'd grow up to look like a fat person they knew who lived nearby. Fiona felt embarrassed and ashamed.

Four years later, almost the exact incident happened again. Fiona went to a party; and again, she drank too much soda, and ate too much food, as well, which again caused her belly to swell and hurt. Just as before, others at the party mocked her. The groundwork for a phobia was now set. The necessary ingredients of fear and guilt were now firmly planted in her subconscious, even though logically forgotten not long afterward.

Ten years later, and Fiona, then seventeen, once more over-indulged in both food and soda at a party. When she complained of stomach pains, someone made an unkind remark about her having a swollen belly. In that instant, the subconscious recalled the childhood trauma and reacted to allay her subconscious fear of developing a large belly. From that day forward, Fiona would experience intense gastrointestinal pain after consuming the smallest amount of food or beverage. An inability to eat or drink would follow. It was her subconscious's way of reminding her of what was said when she was little. Logically, she couldn't remember the two earlier incidents, but the subconscious continued to do all it could to keep her from bloating her belly with food or drink.

When I saw Fiona some six months later, she looked fantastic, healthy and positively radiant! Now that the childhood subconscious trauma had been brought to logical awareness, she could logically deal with the condition and correct it. So much for wanting attention! After a single healing session, plus follow-up care provided by caring therapists, Fiona was able to return to full health.

This was not an isolated case.

Never cause a child to feel guilty about something
they did innocently

A STUDY IN HEALING: UNWANTED ATTENTION

Sally had been through all forms of therapy, some lasting years, to treat her bulimia. Diagnosing her problem, the specialists told her she was "doing it for attention." Can you imagine throwing up day after day, meal after meal, for attention? I can think of more attractive ways of commanding attention! What's more, she was passive in nature; and the last thing she wanted from anyone was attention.

After discussing her history, we began the healing session. Sally quickly regressed to her three-year-old self, and in minutes, she could remember sitting on the floor surrounded by tiny pills. She had taken them from a cupboard.

"What are you doing with the pills?" I asked.

"Eating them," she responded happily.

Sally was eating the pills as if they were candy! She went on to tell me the events that followed. Her mother came into the room and panicked. Sally remembered hearing her mother scream and cry. She began to yell at Sally for being a "naughty girl." Sally was upset and confused. What had she done? Then her father came into the room. Furiously, he commenced yelling at someone over the phone, as Sally's mother became more and more hysterical.

But why were they so mad at her for swallowing something that tasted so good?

Eventually someone came into the room, a doctor I suppose, who gave her something to swallow, which made Sally throw up. Sally's parents became calm. Smiling, they told their daughter what a "good girl" she was. Despite all the confusion, Sally's subconscious did not miss this comment. When Sally swallows something she enjoys, her subconscious notes, she is made to feel frightened and guilty, a "naughty girl"; but when she vomits after swallowing it, she is a "good girl."

In her mid teens, Sally ate some candies her mother was making to include in a cake and was reprimanded for it. Remembering how to correct the guilt, her subconscious initiated vomiting. But the subconscious could not switch the response off as easily as it turned it on. It could only do that after Sally recalled the original cause of her action.

We should be careful about whom we label "attention-seeking" and be thankful that our phobias are not so noticeable.

THE "CLASSICS"

Allergies and eating disorders, while often actually phobias, are not usually recognized as such. But even "classic" phobias are not always what they appear to be.

One such condition is claustrophobia, the fear of being in small places, like elevators or tunnels. I've treated a variety of claustrophobic cases; and although the symptoms are often similar the panic, the anxiety, the causes seem to include a variety of possibilities. I have to keep an open mind about what's going on. An example is a lady who had a fear of flying. On close examination it turned out that she had a fear of being strapped in. As a child she had fallen in her high chair and couldn't get out because of the lap strap.

A STUDY IN HEALING: LOST MOTHER, LOST SON

Cynthia explained that her claustrophobia had crept up on her slowly. At first, without realizing she had a phobia she began to notice that she was avoiding elevators, preferring instead to use the stairs. She also observed that she had taken to carrying a small flashlight with her just in case the elevator lights went out. This made using the elevator easier if stairs were not available and also helped her comfort level when she had to spend time in a small room. But the basic fear of being trapped was still there.

Strangely enough, she enjoyed flying, something many claustrophobics dread because of the confined space within the airplane. So whatever else it might be, her condition wasn't true claustrophobia, which means being afraid of confinement in a small space, *any* small space. And this patient wasn't.

The first memory Cynthia recalled in the healing session was of being trapped under the sheets at the bottom of a bed when she was about three. She recalled her intense panic as she twisted and squirmed, unable to escape because the sheets were so tightly tucked in. I kept her in this situation until the real fear came through: it turned out to be fear not of being trapped under the sheets, but of not knowing where she was. Waking up in the middle of the night and feeling trapped, with no points of reference to establish where you are, can be terrifying.

Cynthia had gone to sleep and woke up feeling restricted, suffocated. But even worse was the feeling of fear and loneliness due to her disorientation at the strange environment.

Cynthia could not work out just what had happened to her, so I regressed her to when she was in her mother's womb. She remembered how calm and peaceful she felt; it was dark and restricted, but she was happy and secure. I then asked her to imagine she was in an elevator that stopped and remained in darkness. This thought caused her no anxiety; the claustrophobia had left. Now all she needed was to be reminded of the security she felt in the womb. Now aware of her real fear, the little girl's fear of not knowing where she was, she was able to put the phobia into an adult perspective; and all her fears evaporated. I often take claustrophobic patients back to a prenatal situation to recall the peace and calm this time of confinement gave, and can still give.

What was most interesting in this case was the trigger that caused the fear to surface later in life. Cynthia had a son who, a year or so earlier had left home. Never sure where he was at any given moment, Cynthia considered the boy "lost." Her subconscious interpretation of her feeling that he was "lost" connected with the childhood incident in which she'd felt lost while trapped in a small place. Once she'd recognized the problem's origin, all she had to do to correct it was to realize that her son was always at the end of a phone, and, therefore, never lost. With this thought, the phobic symptoms disappeared.

This sort of phobic reaction is characteristic of Passive types. They do not do well on their own and often need reassurance about their station in life. When left alone, they easily become insecure, bringing past traumas to the surface.

A STUDY IN HEALING: A MOTHER AND A MOUSE

One of the worst fears children can encounter is to see someone who is responsible for their safety and security lose control. This is a special problem for passive types.

Ann had a fear of mice, not just a nervousness, but a real fear bordering on terror. She had only to see a mouse and would straightway suffer a panic attack.

During our healing session, she went quickly back to a memory of when she was about six years old. Apparently, Ann's mother had a real fear of mice and on this particular day, a mouse ran out from behind a bag while she was sweeping the floor. Well, the moment her mother saw the mouse, she became hysterical. Screaming, yelling, swinging the broom around, she lost all control. Petrified, she didn't know what to do. Eventually, after her husband came in and dealt with the mouse, she calmed down. But little Ann had seen everything.

I asked Ann to imagine that she could still see the mouse. "Yes," she said. I then asked her to pick it up; and with a calm and reassuring voice, I told her that a mouse is only a harmless little animal, with a little heart. "He's frightened just like you," I said. Ann said that she had no difficulty picking up the tiny creature and taking it outside, where it would be free and safe; and in her mind, she did so.

It was at this point that Ann realized her panic in the presence of mice was caused by a fear of her mother's losing control, not by a fear of the animals themselves! Mice only triggered the subconscious memory of her mother's hysteria. After that recognition, Ann no longer feared mice. Few adults realize the intense insecurity children suffer when those who are responsible for their safety panic or lose control. They are unlikely to ever again feel totally safe or secure with that person. Children who have witnessed panic can become withdrawn and nervous due to a feeling of insecurity, particularly the Serious and Passive types.

Children lose their security when adults caring for them show fear

A STUDY IN HEALING: A FORTY-SOMETHING CLIENT, A FOUR-YEAR-OLD SUBCONSCIOUS

Another phobia that I think is fairly common is agoraphobia, a fear of open spaces. This particular client, Alice, had no signs of her phobia until, in her mid-forties, she suddenly found herself beginning to panic every time she left home or walked out of shops into the street. It all began about six months after her father died, and it was generally considered that it was the shock of losing her father that had brought it on. The situation persisted for many years before Alice eventually found her way to my front door. By this time, she had had the usual counseling, drugs and therapy, all to no avail. As she said, the phobia had completely destroyed her enjoyment of life. The point had been reached where she didn't go out anywhere. Her friends no longer called, and it was badly affecting her marriage.

The big difficulty with emotional problems is that they can't be seen. So, unless your friends have experienced it for themselves, there isn't likely to be much sympathy. The usual advice is "Pull yourself together" or "Stop being silly," but this doesn't work because it's our old friend the subconscious taking control of things again. The subconscious has been conditioned by past experience and is immune to logical reasoning.

As Alice's thoughts went back to childhood during the healing, she recalled being around 4-5 years old and in a shopping mall with her father. At some time she remembered looking up and father wasn't there, somehow they had become separated. Her panic started to rise as she wandered around looking for her father. Somehow she walked out into the street and now in full panic wandered around on the side walk trying to find her father. Eventually she saw him, he had come out of the shopping mall looking for his little girl. As soon as she saw him her fear began to subside and her father, in the way typical of parents relieved at finding a child they thought they had lost said, "Where have you been? It's your own fault, you should have stayed with me!"

Now I ask you, was he saying the little 5 year old was somehow more responsible for the situation than he was? But the comment had the desired affect on combining fear and guilt to ensure a future phobia. The type of phobia had yet to be decided and her daddy was just about to do that for her.

Before going further I want to explain that if anyone goes into shock they go into a hypnotic state and whatever is said to someone in a state of shock will come to pass.

Our little girl, Alice, is in deep shock from having been lost when her father takes her to the shopping mall entrance and instructs her, "next time you lose me, don't go outside onto the street, stay indoors where I will know where to find you."

The incident is quickly forgotten, but not by our ever present friend the subconscious who forgets nothing, so when her father dies many years later and a friend asks, "How do you manage now you have lost your father?" her subconscious immediately responds with the thought "Lost father, I mustn't go outside" and so for 10 years her subconscious had faithfully followed father's instructions to stay inside until he found her.

Once the adult she had become was made aware of the child-hood situation which caused the phobia the subconscious gave up its controlling ways and Alice was able to proceed with a normal life.

No matter your age, your subconscious reaction will always be that of the child

MORE PHOBIAS: THE ENDLESS RESOURCEFULNESS OF THE SUBCONSCIOUS

HURTING BY HELPING

Not all phobias are represented as anxiety or panic attacks. The subconscious will use whatever it considers is the most effective means, physical or emotional, in order to prevent the person for whom it is responsible from repeating whatever it was that caused trauma earlier in life.

The subconscious can express its warning in physical terms, sometimes going so far as to maim the body it's supposed to be protecting in order to accommodate programmed emotional needs.

The power of the subconscious to harm
when it means to help is frightening,
and our modern health-care system completely ignores it.

A STUDY IN HEALING: A FEAR OF HUGS

Often, a person's "attitude problem" is in fact a phobic disorder affecting the personality. In Jane's case, her emotional phobia led to a great deal of physical pain.

In her sixties, Jane was afflicted with arthritis, a common ailment of Passive types. On muscle relaxants for years, she couldn't remember a time when she wasn't in stress. Jane's daughter, who had come with her, told me that her mother was in so much pain from her tender joints that she had never been able to hug her children or be hugged by them.

"Oh, that's just me," said Jane. "I feel silly being hugged. I've never liked being hugged or cuddled. I prefer not to be held."

In that last sentence lay the clue. If you are sensitive enough to the deeper thoughts behind a person's comment, you will hear the subconscious telling you what the problem is.

Jane's arthritis was, as she thought, caused by stress, which in turn resulted from a fear of being held close to people or even having an arm put around her. In other words, Jane was suffering from a phobia of being held. Terrified of human contact, she would struggle violently to be free whenever someone tried to put his or her arms around her. Her family, not realizing that this behavior signified an illness, a phobia, had for years teased her about it. But at times, their good humor failed, and they would scold her and accuse her of not loving them. What they were not aware of was Jane's subconscious terror of being held. But why was Jane so scared?

During the healing session, Jane recalled that she had fallen out of her mother's arms when she was only a few months old. In fact, she had been dropped more than once during her childhood, and each time it activated her subconscious into a state of readiness whenever anyone put his or her arms around her. This is why she became so uncomfortable when anyone tried to hug her. Subconsciously she was expecting to be dropped.

A STUDY IN HEALING: OUT OF HER WHEELCHAIR

Unable to stand for more than a few minutes or walk around the house without the aid of crutches, Maureen always used a wheelchair when she traveled away from home. The problem, she told me, was an arthritic spine that affected the strength in her legs. It was on the third visit that I realized I was dealing with a phobia, a deep-seated fear, and that it had nothing to do with her arthritic spine. In fact, Maureen's arthritic spine was also a result of her phobia, as I was able to show her later.

How did I know it was a phobia? That's a bit more difficult to explain, but her conversation and body language, along with my intuition and experience, gave me a clear indication. It began some ten years earlier when her legs had given way after she got out of a car following a long trip. That time, the condition was only temporary, but afterward her back began to ache and her legs became increasingly weaker. Two years later, she was in a wheelchair. Doctors diagnosed her as having an arthritic spine that affected her legs.

During healing, Maureen told me that when she was a little girl she had once climbed out of her bedroom window and slipped on the shingle roof. Fortunately, a friend had grabbed her arm and pulled her back inside, or she would have fallen to the ground. Frightened parents scolded her and blamed her for almost 'killing' herself. Several years later, while crossing a wooden bridge, she suddenly became afraid and got to the other side crawling on her hands and knees. Maureen also told me that as an adult she used to go skiing but was always falling, and her numerous falls were blamed for her arthritic spine.

Her body language led me to the phobia. During healing, she would lean heavily back in her wheelchair but strain to keep her head forward, a classic response to a fear of falling backwards.

I asked her to stand; she told me she would, but only for two or three minutes. I ignored this detail once she was up; and while she was standing, all the information about her past became available. By the time she had finished telling me her story, she had been standing for ten minutes! (In a healing state, one loses all concept of time.) Now I was sure I was dealing with a phobia.

Maureen said she was feeling dizzy and asked if she could sit down. I refused as kindly as possible. We continued talking about her skiing accident. I pointed out that the reason she kept falling while skiing was that her skis were made of wood, just like the shingles on the roof she nearly fell off. Falling backwards had saved her then, so any fear she felt while skiing caused her subconscious to pull her backwards. She had a fear, a phobia, about falling.

At this point, she had been standing for about twenty minutes. Her husband, who was in the room, told me his wife hadn't stood for more than three to four minutes in eight years.

Now, I had to get Maureen walking again. Since the subconscious message had been brought to logical awareness, the phobia had gone; so I took her hand and gently insisted she walk up and down the length of the room with me. I asked her to look ahead, not down. The subconscious will never allow the feet to travel ahead of what it cannot see; so if you watch your feet, you will shuffle and take little steps.

After we'd walked back and forth a few times, I asked her to go with me outside my room into the corridor, and then to the waiting room. She began uncertainly, but as we proceeded down the narrow corridor, her confidence began to return. Maureen was looking ahead, not down, and told me it was a lot easier than she expected. Best of all, she had no pain. Once we got to the door, I decided she should walk to the car. She was on her own now and walked perfectly to where the vehicle was parked. Her husband, deeply emotional, followed with the empty wheelchair. By now, she had been on her feet for forty-five minutes and had walked about seventy to eighty yards, with confidence and mostly without support. Remember, this lady hadn't been able to stand for more than three to four minutes at a time in eight years!

Maureen had endured the gamut of the usual therapies and surgery. If only someone in the medical world had known about body language, eight years of unhappiness could have been avoided.

When a child is in shock, to shout will do more
to cause harm than prevent it.

A RANGE OF REACTIONS

Phobias are about active, physical release such as panic, anxiety attacks, or even, paradoxical though it may seem, inertia. The less confident nature of quiet, passive personalities doesn't allow them to exhibit their fears in a demonstrative way; and so the subconscious produces the non-active symptoms of an allergy.

I have successfully treated people with allergies to gasoline and exhaust fumes by taking them to an original childhood trauma, which usually involves traffic. But the same trauma could just as easily have led to panic or anxiety attacks or, as in one case I recall, asthma attacks. The attacks always came on for John when he went into town, where traffic was more congested than in the sparsely populated area where he resided. He had taken inhalers and steroids for years; but after two healing sessions, his asthmatic reaction to exhaust fumes had disappeared.

The cause of the asthma was a near-accident that took place when John was about seven years old. Had his personality been more aggressive, he would probably have reacted with panic or anxiety attacks once the earlier trauma had been activated. Of course, had he been even less confident and outgoing, he could have reacted with body language even less active than asthma, such as eczema, psoriasis, or any one of a number of skin allergies. Had he been chewing a candy at the time of the trauma, he would have developed an allergy to sugar.

These are typical reactions to childhood trauma. The way to a cure is not to avoid some portion of your diet or close yourself off from your everyday environment. Nor will it help to mask the symptoms with drugs or resort to surgery. The subconscious will only find other ways, other symptoms, of alerting you to the hidden dangers of your situation.

The answer to any phobia is always to find the cause.

A STUDY IN HEALING: DEPRESSED, UNDRESSED

Sometimes, people are misdiagnosed as "depressed" and put onto a course of drugs, when the real reason for their apparent depression or antisocial behavior is no more than a reaction to a childhood trauma.

One such case was a young man who would, with no evident provocation and no sense of embarrassment, take his clothes off in public. After each incident, Robert was treated as a manic-depressive and given psychiatric treatment. He was always depressed when he went through the undressing performance. No one ever thought to treat it as a phobia, which is exactly what it was.

The first time Robert visited me, he recalled being bound tightly when he was tiny. How he hated it! He remembered how he wanted to feel free, to wave his arms and legs about. Instead, he was bound up in such a way that he couldn't move. It was the belief of the time, in the country of his birth, that all babies felt more secure if they were tightly wrapped in shawls. But for this baby, it was a terrible experience. For months he lay in his crib, hot, constricted, and uncomfortable, thinking of nothing else except that he would throw off all tight-fitting clothes when he was old enough to make his own decisions. The time came when the swaddling clothes were left off, and Robert continued to grow like any other child.

Years later, at a discotheque full of wriggling bodies, he became very hot. All of a sudden, he began to feel depressed; and an overwhelming urge to take off all his clothes came over him. Unable to resist, he undressed right in the middle of the disco. He didn't understand why, and he couldn't stop.

Following that first incident, Robert was continually depressed, confused, and disoriented. Doctors diagnosed manic depression, now also called bipolar disorder, and he began disrobing on a regular basis. But his so-called manic depression came to a halt one afternoon in, my office when we started to treat it as a phobia.

Of course not everyone is going to react with feelings of depression, guilt, and rejection just because of a childhood trauma. As we have seen, children react differently to similar situations. The people most likely to react as Robert did are the more sensitive and loving among us. Seriously aggressive children react quite differently. They tend to be defiant and will deliberately repeat what they have been told is wrong, as if to prevent guilt from establishing itself in their thoughts. Less aggressive but still independently minded children tend to keep their emotions hidden. However, they will often take out their feelings on their own children, or on other people around them, later in life.

A STUDY IN HEALING: LOOKING FOR EXTRA ATTENTION

Partially sighted, Audrey could only see images immediately in front of her. Told that her retina cells were not being replaced when the old ones died, she had only slight peripheral vision. She could see detail from six to twelve inches at the most.

Once healing began, she immediately recalled a sense of rejection by her parents. She remembered being a very demanding child, always wanting lots of love and affection. The youngest of several children, Audrey probably wasn't rejected at all. More likely, she was a child whose demands were not recognized and, therefore, could not be met. She was the typical Fun-loving Child.

One day, while the family was traveling in the car, eight-year-old Audrey put on her mother's sunglasses and kept them on for the whole trip. When she got out of the car still wearing the glasses, she had trouble seeing where she was going. So her mother took her hand, something she wouldn't normally do, to guide Audrey.

The little girl loved this extra attention. That night she prayed to be blind so that she could receive more love and attention.

Later in life when she feels she isn't receiving the attention and love she deserves, her subconscious came to her rescue using techniques it learned as a child.

Since the healing session, Audrey's sight has begun to improve. Scary, isn't it?

A STUDY IN HEALING: WRONGLY APPLIED LOVE

The loving, caring father of a family of four children asked if I would help with his eldest son. Anthony was twenty-four and quite unlike the rest of the family: while his brothers and sister were gentle and loving, he was aggressive and disruptive. He was very much loved, but his erratic outbursts of temper kept the family in a state of apprehension.

The boy readily came to see me. He recognized he had a problem and wanted to do something about it. He told me how he had tried to control his quick temper, but couldn't. If the family did anything that he considered stupid, he would rage; if they asked for his advice or for help, he would be short-tempered and sarcastic. Anthony went on to explain that he was totally different with his friends, and had displayed none of the attitude problems at college. Nor did he act up at the job he'd been working at since completing school. It was just at home that he felt different, out of place.

This was another case of love wrongly applied to a small child. When Anthony was about seven or eight years old, his father was away from home a lot; and, as Anthony was the eldest of the children, father would always give him a hug when he was leaving home and tell him to take care of everyone for him while he was away. It was a casual, loving remark meant to imply affection and trust. But the little boy's subconscious took the remark literally.

What a responsibility this was for a boy of seven or eight!

Whatever the other family members did, Anthony would be held responsible. No wonder he reacted with anger when someone did something he thought was wrong. His father's expression of love had encumbered the life of this boy with an incredible burden. Even at twenty-four, his subconscious was still telling him he was responsible for the family. Anthony didn't want this assignment; so at a logical level he reacted with anger to any situation that imposed on him a feeling of responsibility within the family unit, a feeling he did not have when at work or college. Only when he was among his family did his subconscious continue to warn him of the dangers of being responsible for others.

As he began to realize the cause of his problem, a great feeling of delight and relief came over him. He said it was like having a great weight lifted off his shoulders.

"The problem that will follow, of course," he sighed, "is that the family will want to know why I feel better. How can I possibly tell them without causing Dad to feel terribly guilty?"

Children should never be asked to shoulder adult responsibilities

This is one of the problems I faced while writing this book. In outlining how our attitudes toward our children can affect their disposition as adults, I am probably begetting all sorts of guilt complexes in parents who can now see the results of their mistakes.

All I can say about this is not to worry about it.

We all did the best we could with the information available to us at the time.
If this book helps you understand your family a little better, then it has to be good!

Reminders
Allergies and Phobias

An allergy can be an inverted phobia.

Fear compounded by guilt which you cannot remember causes phobias.

Your subconscious mind is always a child and will over-ride your adult logical awareness to act out the childhood beliefs or fears if it thinks you are threatened, .

If you have an irrational thought, ask your subconscious what it is trying to tell you.

Childhood trauma programs the defensive adult.

Never cause a child to feel guilty about something they did innocently.

It is cruel to blame the child for your mistakes.

We all have phobias, some are just more noticeable than others.

Emotional eating disorders are phobias and should be treated as such.

Children lose their security when adults caring for them show fear.

A Helping Hand

The difficulty with emotional problems is that
they can't be seen.

The power of the subconscious to harm when it means
to help is frightening.

An 'attitude' problem can be a phobic disorder.

When a child is in shock, to shout or discipline
will do more to cause harm than prevent it.

Drugs never cure subconscious controlled sickness.
They only suppress it.

The answer to any phobia is to find the cause

Chapter 8

DISCIPLINE

AN ISSUE NOT TO BE DUCKED

By advising parents to understand the individual needs of each of their children, I am not condoning an anything-goes approach in the raising of children. Some parents seem to believe that children should be allowed absolute freedom to express their emotions so as to fully realize themselves as they grow.

What a load of rubbish that belief is!

Even the animal world, which is far more knowledgeable about child rearing than the human world, knows the value of restraint and discipline. In the wild, a creature who is not disciplined in its developmental stage is consigned to an early death, or, at best, a life as an outcast from the flock, herd, or group.

I used to live in a water mill; and as in all such places, several families of wild duck were always present. Each adult pair of mallard had their own personalities and peculiarities, just like any human family. I remember watching a particular mother duck going down the river with her nine ducklings following closely behind. As they approached a bend in the river, one of the ducklings suddenly broke rank and sped forward ahead of all the others, to be first around the bend. When the mother caught up with it, she hit the little duckling so hard across its head with her beak that it was thrown several feet across the river; and I could hear its squeaks of despair above the tumbling of the mill. Mother Duck knew exactly what she was doing. On another occasion, there might have been a heron, a stoat, or some other danger lurking around the bend in the river, which would have resulted in the precocious duckling's death. One thing was certain, that little duck wouldn't risk its life in that way again.

I've watched the way different ducks manage their families. Some are conscientious and strict, never letting the little ones out of their sight. Most of their brood survived. Other ducks are lazy. They do nothing to discipline their family or keep it together, so that the brood scatters over a large area of the river. These ducks usually lose most of their ducklings within a few weeks.

Exactly the same is true of human families. Children need to know the extent of their freedom. .

Children need boundaries or rules
within which they can feel safe and secure.

SURVIVAL IS TAUGHT

Undisciplined children are insecure. I knew of an eighteen-year-old boy who had never been taught to accept the word "No." All his life, he had been allowed to have and to do whatever he wanted. Then came that great moment in his life when someone finally did say "No!" It was a girl he wanted to date. He went into shock, threatening suicide and other forms of retribution if he couldn't have his way. But that big "No!" persisted. At the height of his emotional trauma, he put a plastic bag over his head to frighten the girl into satisfying his demands. Minutes later he was dead. If only someone had said "No" when he was weeks and months old and not given in to his every demand.

Happiness is a key to survival. Without discipline for personal welfare and security, happiness is soon lost. Survival may not mean the same to the human individual as it does to a wild animal; but without the emotions of happiness and freedom within well-defined boundaries of discipline, survival hasn't much meaning.

I am not suggesting any form of violence towards children or anyone else. I am opposed to violence. *Totally.* Nonetheless, a baby of a few weeks old is quite capable of knowing what it can get away with and what it cannot. Be firm with your baby in the early months and you will be more likely to have a child who loves within the family. If you allow children to have their own way all the time, they will prove to be a source of unending discord. Self-expression is not necessarily good.

*All children have to learn the rules of a civilized society
at some stage in their life; for their own sake, as well as yours,
the earlier the better.*

INTRODUCING CHILDREN TO THE ADULT WORLD

Try as they may, parents cannot change what's out there in the world their children will inherit. Violence, deprivation, and fear are all too real; children need to be introduced to the knowledge of it gradually.

This is where nursery rhymes and fairy tales have their place. Children need to be introduced to the hurt and rejection of life in ways that causes them no psychological harm. Stories of giants (all adults are giants to children), wicked fairies, punishment, and even violence, as in "Tom and Jerry" cartoons and other innocent stories, all serve to slowly and deliberately introduce children to an adult world without instilling fear or guilt in their minds. The *sudden* introduction to fear and guilt caused by adult films, even nonviolent ones, cause the subconscious to overreact and create defense mechanisms that will plague children as they go through life.

Many child psychologists object to fairy tales and cartoons like "Tom and Jerry" because of the violence and gender typing. But children must be introduced slowly to comedy and humor as well as hurt and fear.

Sudden jolts of reality drive the subconscious into a defense mode.
It needs to develop gently.

NOT A TIME TO INTERFERE

It is very tempting to step in and separate children when they argue with comments such as, "stop arguing, stop being silly." When parents intervene between arguing siblings all they do is postpone the disagreement until the youngsters find another time or place when the parent can't overhear. There is nothing wrong in sibling rivalry and as long as it doesn't get out of hand it is best for the parent to stay out of it. Children learn conversational tactics for both defense and attack in their discussions and arguments. If a parent continually interferes to stop children vying with each other in discussion, they grow to become adults unable to debate a subject effectively. They will not have learned in their younger years how to react with spontaneous replies.

You can always tell when an adult was prevented from active, aggressive dialogue. They don't know how to verbally defend themselves. In their subconscious mind they hold back, waiting for the parent to intervene for them or fearful that if they aggressively defend themselves some adult will step in and blame them for the disturbance. I have seen many adults who because they are the eldest of the family, are unable to defend themselves in verbally abusive situations such as at meetings. This is because being the oldest they usually were blamed if there was an argument. Parents have a tendency to protect the youngest and weakest against their more eloquent and stronger older brothers and sisters. If this is done too often, the younger child will use it as a tactic against the older one who will find it easier to say nothing than get into trouble defending themselves.

PARENTS SHOULD NOT UNNECESSARILY INTERFERE IN SIBLING RIVALRY

Children argue and tease in a different way to adults. They are testing each other, learning how to defend and compete. They are teaching each other the art of spontaneous response. Should the parent decide to join in they are more likely to limit discussion and the art of dialogue than help it. Children will not compete with their parents in discussion. Children need to be allowed to practice conversation between themselves. If you listen in on your children's conversations, you will be impressed at the arguments that come up; and don't expect the baby of the group to be left out. They are often the most vocal, having had to fight for every piece of attention or space within the children's world.

The wonderful thing about conversation is that it carries energy and attention. Children feed on the thoughts within the energy and from this process originality grows. Open discussion between children challenges them to compete with each other and to be original. Children often resent adults interfering in their world of thoughts.

Leave your children to argue in peace.
If you interfere you will be disturbing a valuable lesson.

DON'T SHOUT BACK

Have you ever wondered what to do when your child comes home upset, angry and refuses to do as you ask, or perhaps the child attacks you verbally using bad language and tells you they don't love you? It's surprising how quickly the 4 to 6 year old will pick up bad language. Most parents try to control the situation with discipline of some form. After all you can't have a youngster coming home and shouting abuse at mother.

This is not the time to get tough. This is the time to get down on your knees and take the little one into your arms. Something has obviously happened that has upset them very deeply and your shouting and trying to prevent this uncalled for out burst of bad behavior is only going to cause them to internalize the problem. The last thing you want is for your child to have problems that they feel they cannot share with you.

'Problems internalized eventually become health problems
or 'uncontrollable rage.'

I realize that it is upsetting to have a youngster shouting at you but try to understand that your child is not upset with you. Your child is not seeing you when their rage releases itself. In an atmosphere of love and security, which is what home should always be, we feel safe to release our inner thoughts and feelings. Your child, returning to the safety of home after a particularly bad day at school where he might have been teased or bullied by older children or thinks, usually wrongly, that the teacher is singling him out as an example, feels safe to release the pent up hurt that has been building during the day. It isn't you, the parent, he is angry with, but the unseen teacher or children that he couldn't deal with at school.

In this situation their need is for love, not discipline. Put your arms around the little one and tell them how much you love them. If they kick and scream and shout, it doesn't matter. They are learning that it is safe to bring their problems to you. Continue to hold and love them. Eventually the anger will change to crying, then sobbing as they release the loneliness and hurt suffered at school.

I don't care how long it takes, or if the meal is spoiling.

A child in anger is a child in need of love
And they need it now,

not at some later time at your convenience. After the sobbing has released the hurt they will return your loving concern for their unhappiness with hugs and a kiss and then as suddenly as they erupted in anger, they will move from you to play or get something to eat. Now is not the time to question them about the problems that led to the anger. They will confide in you when they are ready.

Never pressure children to confide in you,
all you do is force them to internalize their problems.

To pressure a child into telling you what is wrong will not be seen as loving concern, but will be felt as insensitivity to their feelings. If they know they are loved they will come to you for help if they need it.

When you are sensitive to a child's emotions to be left alone, loved, or guided, they will respond with love and come to trust and confide in you.

An angry child is an unhappy child.
In the presence of love, a child's anger dissolves.

Children will not confide in an adult who pressures them to release the reason for their unsociable behavior. To force a child to release information to satisfy your curiosity will be seen as rejection, not love. When they do eventually come to you with their fears and unhappiness, listen to what they have to say. Don't jump in with your own anger telling them what they should have done. When a child confides in you there are three golden rules;

Listen, Listen, Listen

'It is comfort and love they first need, not a lecture.'

If they think they are going to get a lecture every time they come to you with problems they will cease to confide in you. They already know they didn't handle the situation well and confirming it for them isn't going to help their self esteem. When you listen they feel comforted and secure.

Don't offer children advise on how to deal with other children unless they ask for your help.

When children are in trouble, it's your love they want, not your criticism.

If after the child has told you what caused their anger you also become angry, the child will feel guilty for upsetting you. If the parent shows distress at information confided to them by the child, the child will cease to confide in the parent. Your distress at their difficulties creates guilt within the child's mind.

Children lose their sense of security when parents over react.

Reminders
Discipline

Children should never be asked to shoulder adult responsibilities.

Children need boundaries and rules within which they can feel safe and secure.

Children need to know the extent of their freedom.

Undisciplined children are insecure.

Without discipline for personal welfare and security, happiness is soon lost.

All children have to learn the rules of a civilized society at some stage in their life. For their sake as well as yours, the earlier the better.

Our learning years are to help us find our potential in happiness.

Sudden jolts of reality drive the subconscious into defense mode. It needs to develop gently.

Most children are not naturally naughty. They just don't understand what you want.

Allow your children to argue in peace.
If you interfere you will be disturbing a valuable lesson.

A Helping Hand

A child in anger is a child in need of love and they need it now, not at some later time at your convenience.

Never pressure children to confide in you,
all you do is force them to internalize their problems.

In the presence of love, a child's anger dissolves.
An angry child is an unhappy child.

Children will not confide in an adult who pressures them
to release the reason for their unsociable behavior.

Don't offer children advice on how to deal with
other children unless they ask for your help.

When they are in trouble,
it's your love they want, not your criticism.

Children lose their sense of security when parents over-react.

CHAPTER 9

ENERGY
The Fuel of Life

ELECTRICALLY DRIVEN

I think all parents are aware of the drain that children are on the adults around them but I don't think many people realize just how essential to the child's health and happiness their energy is. Energy is an electromagnetic force sometimes referred to as bio-energy. It is a force that pulsates throughout the body; without it life cannot exist. It is this bio-energy, which stimulates cell division, chemical release and a whole host of other physical and mechanical reactions within the body. Chemicals are secondary in importance to electrical stimulation.

To fully understand our children and ourselves we need a basic understanding about how this life sustaining force works, where it comes from and how it affects our thinking, health and happiness. Energy comes from the sun, which is one reason why the Egyptians and other earlier civilizations were sun worshipers. They were aware that light equals life and that the body converts sunlight into energy. The ultimate in converting sunlight to bio-energy is a reptile, but to a greater or lesser extent we are all sun dependent.

Fortunately for us, plants also convert the sun's rays into energy in the form of sugar. We then eat these plants in their various states and convert the many forms of sugars back into bio-energy. From this we get the fuel of life that we need for existence.

There is a third form of energy available and that is the surplus and radiating energy of the people around us. This has nothing to do with spiritual energy, which is of a totally different source and not part of this discussion. All of us radiate energy and it can be measured and even photographed. The strength of this radiating bio-energy depends upon the health of the individual, their own needs and the surplus energy they have after their own needs have been met.

The value of this surplus energy to others is very much dependent upon individual attitudes. Negative energy has very little value for anyone. The body needs a constant supply of positive energy on which to function and operate successfully. Those with a surplus of positive energy will pass it to those with less. Negative people or people with less energy than they need for daily living will draw positive energy from others. Positive energy increases cell bonding, faster healing and recovery from shock. Negative energy has an opposing affect.

TWO'S A CROWD

With these facts in mind, let's start with the pregnant mother and her unborn child. In the early stages of fetal development there is an explosion of cell development. As I said earlier it is energy pulsing through a cell that causes it to divide and multiply. Therefore in the early months of pregnancy a mother's need for energy is incredible. The growing child will remain dependent for energy on mother and then other members of the family for many years to come. The child is unable to produce for itself all the energy it needs for health, growth and development and for that reason will continue to be a drain on the adults around them for years. Exactly how long they will continue to be a drain on parents depends on many factors, one of which is how quickly you teach them to be independent in thought and action.

This is one of the reasons why grandparents find their grand-children tiring. As people get older they have less energy and are therefore unable to meet the constant demands for energy that children require. Then as a subconscious defense mechanism their patience dwindles if the child becomes demanding.

Of course the point at which we reach old age is very much dependant upon the individual. I remember one lady who at 90 used to tell me that she couldn't stay talking with me for long because she had to go around the village to see to the needs of the 'old dears' as she used to call them. "How old are these people you look after?" I once asked. "Oh, in their seventies and eighties." she replied as she got on her bike to go on her travels.

If children annoy you, it maybe because you are not as fit as they are and therefore they are innocent of any wrongdoing.

DEPENDENCE

Babies needs more than just their mother's milk. They also need her energy. For nine months baby has been totally dependent upon mother for this life sustaining energy, now suddenly it is thrust into the big world and separation from mother and her energy is life's first big trauma. In those early hours, days and weeks separation means stress, another word for energy depletion. The baby's survival system quickly learns to absorb the energy it needs from mothers milk. Mother's milk is supplying more than just nutrients, she is also supplying life-sustaining energy. When baby cries it is because he or she wants to be held, assuming it has no other problems. Holding, nursing allows a transfer of energy from one to the other. If for some reason mother is short of energy or if the available energy is very negative, baby is likely to be restless, perhaps cry a lot and require a lot of attention. Babies are in harmony with their mother's energy when they are born and will continue to remain so unless there is separation between them before baby has developed sufficiently to start the process of independent thinking.

Some babies, of course, seem to need more attention than others and this is the first time we begin to see an attitude pattern. Some babies are very quiet and controlled; are these going to be the serious type, (independent and self-sufficient) already producing the energy they need for themselves? Some babies are very demanding, needing to be picked up and held. Are these going to be attention seeking, controlling little people? And of course, some babies just seem to be too good to be true, undemanding, quiet and seemingly happy to be left alone, even though they probably feel lonely and neglected. Instead of complaining when you come, they are happy to see you. Are these babies going to become the undemanding passive children?

In whichever way your baby reacts be sure of one thing, it has a need to be loved and held, to be in your presence for many months to come.

BONDING

Some children lose the ability to attract energy very early on. There must be many reasons for this but one could a separation from mother without explanation. Imagine for a moment that you are a baby again. You have been dependent upon mother's life sustaining energy for nine months, or longer. You are then suddenly taken from your mother, no explanation is given, you are not sure when or even if ever you will be allowed back. What do you do now? Your subconscious takes over and you begin to produce energy for yourself. Of course, to do so your little brain has to work overtime. It has to race to keep up with the demand the ever-growing body makes on it for energy. Believing it is unable to rely on the parent for it's energy, baby will develop an independence that will not include you in its thinking patterns. In fact, the child will be unable to utilize your energy when you are reunited. Bonding will have been broken.

A new situation has been created. Baby's mind is now into permanent racing speed to keep up with the demand for energy. You have a hyper-active (ADHD) child to deal with.

Broken bonding can cause ADD, ADHD

FUEL CRISIS

This is one reason why hyper-active children crave sugar. Unable to utilize the radiating energy of others, their minds have to race to produce thought-induced energy. They are short of energy. I realize that this line of thinking goes contrary to the current medical opinion but in the majority of cases it is not a chemical deficiency that is causing your child's hyper-activity, but an energy deficiency. It is because of this they grow up craving sugar. I accept that there could be other reasons why they are short of energy, but there is no doubt in my mind, having treated many children with this difficulty, that energy deprivation is the cause of their constant activity. They cannot switch off. So deprived are they of energy that they constantly crave an alternative energy source, sugar. I am not saying that refined sugar is necessarily good for them, but they do need an alternative source of energy. I have found that glucose is an excellent alternative to refined sugar and some 80% of the children I help with this problem benefit from the extra energy.

Children and adults often have difficulty sleeping if their energy levels are too low. Think about it for a minute. We need energy to keep the heart beating, the lungs pumping and all the other millions of things that keep the body going. When we sleep the body relies on the surplus energy we have stored in various parts of the body during the day. But what if we haven't been able to store a surplus? It then becomes impossible to sleep because the brain cannot switch off. It has to keep powering energy through the body. In this situation we either don't go to sleep, or wake up early in the morning unable to get back to sleep or dream all night as the brain keeps ticking over.

Just as thirst implies a need for water,
a need for sweet things implies a need for energy.

LEARNING

Shortage of energy affects children's health and happiness, it also affects learning and sporting abilities. One of the functions of the brain besides being a complex chemical factory and electrical generator is to act as the body's computer. Like any other computer it receives and stores information and when required, releases it as memory. But like any other computer it needs electricity pulsed through it at the right frequency before it will function properly. It therefore follows that if your children have energy depletion they will have learning difficulties. I'm not referring to children with known intellectual response diffi-culties, though often these can be enhanced with extra intakes of energy, but normal children who for a variety of reasons will be low on energy. When energy is low concentration and compre-hension become difficult. On the other end of the continuum, recall of information also becomes difficult. Low energy affects intellectual ability. If your child needs sugar, allow them access to glucose. The effect is amazing. Stressed out children relax and concentration, comprehension and memory recall enhance grades, improved good health is maintained and happiness ensued.

I know of one student who always carried glucose around with her and just before class and more particularly before an exam, she would chew on a glucose tablet. The effect this had on her was so obvious to others that it wasn't long before she was supplying her friends with glucose.

The reasons for low energy levels are many,
but the result is always the same: STRESS,
less happiness, poor health, and low academic standards.

TOO CRAMMED TO EMPTY

A small point here while discussing exams. I will never understand why students of any age are encouraged to read and study information until the final hour before the exam. This is terribly wrong. Your computer needs time to adjust from taking in and storing information to searching for and releasing it. If the student has been cramming until the final day it is unlikely to be able to reverse the programmed attitude in the short space of a few hours. Absorbing information requires different responses to the one that releases information flow. It takes time to adjust thought processes, especially ones as opposite as learning and applying. The student needs to be discussing and talking about the examination subjects at least several days before the exam and preferably several weeks. The more they are encouraged to discuss the subject detail with friends and family the easier it will be to recall the detail when needed.

We learn as much listening to ourselves
as we do listening to others.

WHO IS TEACHING WHO

It would be arrogant to believe that one short book could somehow be sufficient to outline the responsibilities of parents towards their children.

Thousands of books have been written on the subject and parents spend a lifetime learning about the tasks needed to fulfill the role of parenting. If you have more than one child you will have spent more than one life time learning about the intricacies of guiding a life through the sunshine and the blizzards of its journey.

Being a parent is not easy, but neither should it be looked

on as a heavy responsibility. All it needs is an understanding of your child's unique needs and abilities and a lot of common sense. A relationship between parent and child is unique. No two situations being the same even within the family as no two personalities are the same. Any guide lines on parenting, and they can be no more than guide lines, must be interpreted using a lot of common sense to suit the particular situation. Every child needs to be loved, but they won't all need that love to be displayed or administered in the same way. Some will enjoy the silence of love, a smile, an arm around the shoulder, your presence in time of need, but without your involvement in their needs.

Others will need a demonstrative show of affection, verbal approval and a more physical involvement in their longings, desires and disappointments. But *NEVER* should the advice found in books such as this one and the multitude of magazines on sale proffering advise and guidance on parenting, be taken literally. The only person who can fully understand the relationship between you and your child is you and even that comes second to the child's understanding of itself.

Parents are there to guide and direct their children in the maintenance of self respect and any word, thought or deed which removes from a child their self respect is to be avoided at all times.

No one has the right to remove self respect from any person,
even more so from a child.

WE WERE NEVER LIKE THAT!

Children should not be encouraged to be like other members of the family. To set standards of behavior, within acknowledged moral and social rules is essential but the learning child should not be admonished for mistakes innocently made any more the parent should feel guilty for parenting mistakes innocently made. As we enter into this chapter on *'Do's and Don'ts'* I want you to keep an open mind, remembering it can be no more than a guide, that parenting is a joy and an honor not a burden or task. That you, like your child, will make mistakes as you learn together the joy of a sharing and growing relationship based on the love which can only be experienced within a family grouping. Never mold your children to be as your expectations of them, but be aware of their expectations of you to guide them, with love to being independent, capable adults building their own foundations for life which must be separate though, hopefully, integrated with yours.

Be aware of your children's expectations of you.

RESPONSIBILITY IS TAUGHT

If your teenage children have been allowed to have free run of the house without feeling any responsibility for maintaining it they will have cause to view it more as a bed and breakfast service than a commune.

Every family should be a commune.
Sharing is fun.

If sharing family responsibilities has not been part of their childhood education a certain selfishness in the attitudes of the youngsters will have developed.

For example, they will expect to be able to take the car whenever it suits them at no cost and probably not replace the gas they use. This can't be allowed to go on for when they no longer need your bed and breakfast service they will only think of you as a provider. This level of selfishness is not good for anyone. Youngsters need to be taught that parents also have needs which need to be respected.

Ask them to wash and clean the car or mow the lawn. If they refuse to accept the responsibility don't argue or be a martyr to the cause, just wait until they need the car and tell them casually it will cost them $X for the evening and they must return it with a full tank of gas. If they want to invite their friends around for a party expecting you to clean up after them and provide the food, give them an estimate of the costs., explaining that its cash in advance.

A bit of reality in the child goes a long way to developing a
sense of responsibility in the adult.

Reminders
Energy

Bio-electricity is the fuel of life.

Positive energy is life enhancing.
Negative energy is life threatening.

Negative people take energy from more positive types.

Babies are dependent on mother's energy in the early months after birth.

Children need an adult's positive energy to thrive.

If children are too demanding in their need for energy, adults will push them away.

If children annoy you it maybe because you are not as fit as they are and therefore they are innocent of any wrong doing.

Hyper-active children are short of energy.

Just as thirst implies a need for water, a need for sweet things implies a need for energy.

If energy is low, it is more difficult to sleep.

Low energy affects retention and release of information.

A relationship between parent and child is unique.

A Helping Hand

No one has the right to remove self respect from
any other person, even more so a child.

Children should never be encouraged to be like other
members of the family.

A child should not be admonished for mistakes innocently
made any more than the parent should feel guilty for
mistakes innocently made.

Be aware of your children's expectations of you.

Every family should be a commune, sharing is fun.

A bit of reality in the child goes a long way to developing
a sense of responsibility in the adult.

Chapter 10

REJECTION

I AM AS I AM

Any form of rejection towards another person, irrespective of age, though dependent on personality, will cause the person to reject themselves. Why do people find it necessary to see fault in others when there is none?

The most important aspect of parenting is to develop and maintain within the child and eventually the adult an awareness of self respect. Any attitude of rejection, such as 'you look fat in that,' is immediately interpreted as 'I'm fat and not acceptable for who I am.' 'I am not acceptable being me,' or 'I don't look nice.' Rejection, or what the child thinks is rejection is one of the biggest causes of mal adjustment in the mature adult causing all sorts of health and emotional difficulties. Rejection is often well advanced before the child is born. Don't have any doubt in your mind that your child is aware of focusing on your thoughts and actions many months before its birth. I have regressed far too many adults back to pre birth situations to find the cause of their difficulties to have any doubts in my mind that rejection is for the newly born, one of the bigger problems.

Reject the infant and the infant will first reject itself and later you.

To be rejected at birth is a terrific trauma. Some babies know in advance of birth that they are unwanted, either because the parent wants the opposite sex of what the baby knows it is going to be or because the baby knows it isn't wanted in any form.

I have had adults who believe 'I'm not good enough' or 'I'll never be perfect' because the pregnant mother constantly worried that her unborn child might not be perfect, physically, but that was interpreted by the child as 'not good enough.' The trauma is terrific, no wonder many babies struggle against birth for this child's life starts devoid of self respect and in fear. How can the child have self respect if it believes it is the wrong sex, imperfect or perhaps shouldn't even be there. When the growing child and then adult are unable to believe in their own worth they discard themselves, hold back, believing others are more worthy. Any comment by a family member, doctor, nurse such as 'what a big nose this baby has.' will create a phobia within the child's thinking which will cause it to feel distress about it's looks for the rest of its life. Of course the child and adult will never be able to reason why they feel inferior.

As you will have noticed from earlier chapters, a lack of self worth is a particular problem for the more sensitive child who has a fear of disapproval. Rejection, associated with a lack of self worth, limits ability and achieving full academic potential. It is also impossible to be totally happy and care free if you don't like yourself for who you are. If you don't like yourself you send out energy as body language preventing anyone else liking you. It doesn't matter how much you love your children, if you consistently adopt an attitude which is disapproving or critical you will cause them to lose confidence and when that happens they eventually begin to feel inferior.

Happiness cannot be experienced in an attitude of self doubt or inferiority.

PROTECTED

House rules should be worked out in advance, not made up as you go along so that the child is never sure if what they are doing will cause your disapproval. Discipline is to maintain a set of family standards which need to be attainable and to the benefit of the child and family harmony. If the discipline is there to make life easier for you it will quickly fall apart.

Children want to be part of the family, not separated from it by rules of convenience.

Children know when family rules are for the good of all and are then eager to participate. It is rejection when there are no rules and the child is free to live its own life, creating its own standards. There is no security in this. Rules, boundaries, mean you care and that the rules are there to assure family harmony. If there are no rules, if children believe the adults around them are uninterested in what they do or how they do it, they come to think no one cares. This is rejection. Even when you smother them with love, they will not believe it if they don't feel safe within boundaries. Is it any wonder that there are so many parents who are at a loss to understand why their children seem to reject them? 'But I gave them everything,' claim the parents. Yes, everything except a sense of protection and security. This is interpreted as rejection. When children are restricted from having all they want because it is not in the interests of all the family members or others would be deprived by their gain, the child will feel included and accepted as part of a larger unit. Children also have a need to give, to contribute.

A child who is given everything believes itself superior and will not adjust to live or work in harmony with others. This is not a way to foster a need for thinking of others. I realize that it's hard on many parents to say no. They don't like to feel rejected by the child and so will do almost anything to satisfy the child's wants in order to have their approval.

Children are not there to satisfy a parent's need for acceptance. Parents are there to satisfy a child's needs for love, security and happiness.

In early learning years most children will do almost anything to avoid being rejected.

Rejection should never be used as a way to apply discipline. If the child feels rejected it will have little interest in your opinions later in life and will not be over concerned for your approval, or the approval of society. It has already learned rejection by the family it loves.

Rules and boundaries which apply equally to all siblings and which are clearly communicated and explained will be accepted. Of course they will test you, try and break the rules. In this they are testing your strength of character. They will feel annoyed and restricted, but they will also feel secure and loved, cared for and confident. A child who is free within boundaries of rules, which are explained as the child learns responsibility, will grow up secure within itself knowing it is accepted. Children rarely break rules to annoy the parent if they grew up within a loving atmosphere of family harmony. No child will deliberately cause itself to be rejected, but if it feels rejected by default they will often purposefully do things which shock you, just to get your attention. Attention as disapproval is better than no attention at all.

A child learns to accept itself and love itself in giving, and being part of your boundaries. A child which is made to feel it is responsible for the family's status at school or at work rejects itself if it doesn't achieve what it believes are your standards.

The child quickly learns to reject itself
if it thinks this will earn your approval.

Reminders
Rejection

It is rejection when you try to change your child's character,
Instead of molding it.

Always maintain within the child an awareness of self respect.

Rejection is one of the biggest causes of maladjustment
in the adult.

Rejection at birth is the biggest rejection of all.

Critical comments about the child, to the child, instead
of explanation, will cause distress and low self esteem.

Happiness cannot be experienced in an attitude
of self doubt or inferiority.

Discipline is to maintain a set of family values which
need to be attainable and to the benefit of family harmony.

Children want to be part of the family, not separated
from it by rules of convenience.

A child who is given everything believes itself superior and will
not adjust to live or work in harmony with others. It is rejection
when you exclude the child from your world of denial.

Rejection

Children are not there to satisfy a parent's need for acceptance. Parents are there to satisfy a child's needs for love, security and happiness.

In the early years most children will do almost anything to avoid being rejected.

If you laugh at a child causing them to feel rejected they will have little interest in your opinions later in life.

Children rarely break rules to annoy the parent if they grow up within a loving atmosphere of family harmony.

A child learns to accept itself and love itself in giving.

Children need attention and attention gained through disobedience is often better than no attention at all.

Children who feel rejected will eventually reject those who were their teachers.

Chapter 11

Guilt

WHO, ME?

Strange, isn't it, but when the adult makes a mistake involving a child they nearly always blame the child. If the child gets lost it has to be the child's fault so when the frightened child is found the first words of comfort he is likely to hear are 'where have you been?' 'It's your own fault, you should have stayed with us.' Now I ask you, how can a little 5 year old possibly be to blame or even guilty of blame at all? Isn't it more likely that it's the adult who is to blame, unless of course they are so incapable of responsible action that the child must cover for the adult.

Every time the child is made to feel guilty
more of its confidence is lost

until eventually the child loses all self respect and confidence. 'Now look what you've made me do,' says mother as she knocks something over. 'My fault again' thinks the child, 'I'm just no good, I make mother unhappy and cause her to make mistakes. I'm in the way.' Soon the child believes that they must shoulder responsibility for the well being of all the family.

Children should never be made to feel responsible for what the parents have or have not done. One of the things many adults have to learn is to be responsible for their own situation in life. We are all responsible for our own happiness or lack of it and complaining about a situation in front of the child, and especially to the child, causes them to think they are in some way guilty for the parents' unhappiness. For what other reason would the parent complain to them, is the subconscious thought running through their minds.

If you are constantly complaining about the housework or the gardening, the child will begin to feel guilty about your situation. This leaves the child with three options:

1) Remove themselves from the situation as soon as they can. This is more the response of Serious children. You are basically driving the child from your life because the serious children will remove themselves from negative situations.

2) The child, feeling guilty because of the complaining parent, will begin to take responsibility for the situation. No child likes to see a parent unhappy and the Passive child, especially, with their guilt loaded emotions will abandon their own life to try and improve the parents'.

3) The third option is to completely ignore the situation and internalize the emotions of the parent resulting in illness at a later date. Fun-loving children will quickly learn how the guilt laden comments are being used to control others and will

eventually use the same tactics themselves and thus begin another generation of complaining adults with psychosomatic illnesses.

A parent has a responsibility to bring happiness into a child's life, protecting them from adult difficulties and stress. They will learn soon enough for themselves about the difficulties of life and if you are always complaining about your problems they will not confide their problems to you. Children have no desire to add to a parent's weight of responsibility, especially if they are made to feel guilty about it.

> *Complaining about life in front of your children,*
> *makes them feel responsible for the situation.*

MORAL BLACKMAIL

Some adults have so perfected the art of dispensing guilt that they use it throughout the lives of their children to control them and, if they can get away with it, they use the same tactics to control others. We call it moral-blackmail. It is a strategy to control others so that they become no more than slaves to the parent they serve. Long before the child has matured they have come to know that unless they give constant attention to the demanding parent they will be made to feel guilty for the parents situation or emotions. Remarks such as 'After all I have done for you', 'Looking after you is so tiring', or 'You are never here to help me.' are guilt loaded statements meant to hurt causing the child to become into line. Comments such as 'when you do that you make Mommy unhappy' is aimed right at the child's guilt center. I have heard teachers say to children 'you shouldn't do that, it will hurt your parents.' Guilt loaded sentiments such as these do nothing to raise confidence and self respect in the child. The stronger child will ignore the self pity and when old enough will move away. The more sensitive, caring child will become your prisoner.

Guilt, as a form of control is insidious and evil. It robs the child of any degree of independence. At the back of the child's mind will always be the thought 'am I going to be made to feel bad because of this?' Any line of reasoning which is based on insinuating guilt parading as love to control another human being is about as bad as it gets. It robs the growing child of their independence.

I accept that when children do things which they know are wrong they have to accept accountability for their actions. But never give them reason to believe that you have been hurt because they exercised independence.

Children want to volunteer their help with thoughts of love.
Not be forced to care with guilt and shame.

The attention so gained isn't love, it's servitude, born out of a loss of self respect.

Reminders
Guilt

Every time the child is made to feel guilty
more of its confidence is lost.

Complaining of their past mistakes is controlling
with guilt and they will resent you because of it.

Using guilt to control is moral blackmail.

Guilt as a form of control is insidious and evil.

Thoughts of guilt rob the growing child of independence.

Refrain from using such phrases as,
      'You are driving me crazy,'
      'You should be ashamed of yourself,'
      'I'm here on my own all day,' etc.

Your are controlling with guilt when your children do things
for you because they feel obliged to do them.

Children should never be made to feel responsible
for your emotions.

CHAPTER 12

FEAR

IT'S A GOOD RESULT BUT.....

Children should be allowed to grow up in an atmosphere that is free of fear. One of the responsibilities of being a parent is to provide a safe, secure haven for their children, one in which they are taught the rules of shared responsibility, love, understanding and consideration for others. Unfortunately too many children only experience fear. I'm not referring to the fear of sexual, physical or verbal abuse. These atrocities are obvious enough. It would be wrong to ignore the fact that these abuses exist, but it is not the purpose of this short narrative on parenting to deal with a subject that is so obviously wrong. I am concerned with the more subtle and often innocently induced conditions of fear.

Children are born with a desire to love and to be loved, to please and to be accepted. Nothing gives a child greater joy than being able to do something for a parent which is accepted with love and happiness. But all too often the child's efforts to please are criticized and what started out as an activity of pleasure becomes a duty of pressure. I remember seeing one little boy trying his hardest to tie his own shoe laces. His mother, instead of encouraging with loving attention said, 'You are not trying hard enough." You could see the look of disappointment written all over his face. This little boy was in a situation where it didn't matter how hard he tried it was never going to be good enough. Listening to his mother it would be hard to believe she was talking to a 3 year old. When children are trying their hardest and struggling to do their best and all they get is criticism they will stop trying.

If their best is not good enough why bother to please?

Of course if they are afraid of your reaction because of your impatience which is threatening in some way, they will go to the limits of their abilities in an emotion of fear. Fear replaces love. If you cause fear in one area of their lives it will spread into other areas of activity and the child becomes fear driven. A fear driven child often becomes a fear driving adult. Driven and pressured by fear as a child, because of the parents impatience the child learns to know of no other way to get what it needs and so enforces fear in others. These children grow without knowing gentleness or complete happiness. The emotion of fear is too deep in their emotions and stress is a constant factor in their lives.

Children who grow up learning how to deal with life's problems through a barrage of criticism instead of love soon develop an anticipation of criticism. They fear that no matter what they do it will not be good enough. Comments such as 'is that the best you can do?' 'You didn't try hard enough,' soon replace confidence and enthusiasm with fear and low self esteem. In an atmosphere of criticism it becomes easier to stop trying than risk attracting more criticism.

Fear of failure is a very real problem for many of today's youngsters who are expected to be perfect in everything from science through art to philosophy. There is no room for failure. The parents are so concerned about their own measurement of success that they fail to see the child's successes or happiness in a situation. They look for failure as if they need to have something to criticize. Fear of this sort comes from all sources; parents, teachers and others who are more interested in academic or sporting success than happiness. A parent is there to instill confidence with loving encouragement and happiness at the child's attempts to please.

The aim should be to prevent or remove fear.

***Anyone who puts fear into the heart of another
is a menace in society.***

Why do adults think it funny to tease children? As I pointed out in early chapters, teasing very often leads to phobias, phobias such as anorexia. I remember a woman who had a fear of heights because an uncle had jokingly threatened to throw his little niece out of the top of a building if she didn't smile for the camera. Then there is the case of a man who had a fear of snakes because some fool relative had held him close to a harmless snake when he was little, thinking how funny it was to see the little boy squirm in fear and then shouting at him for being silly. Even tickling children, if taken too far, can be a form of child abuse. I have had people who didn't like to be touched which went back to being tickled when they were little.

Any action or situation which innocently or deliberately causes fear in the thoughts and emotions of children is abuse and will rob the child of their confidence and self respect.

Children need to be trained to read, write, use a fork, dress themselves and later to study and learn. But fear should never be the instrument used to 'encourage' the desired result. Fear robs the child of happiness and the desire to do well. When the child needs to please the parent because they fear the parent or the parent's reaction, they will feel unloved. The child may still love the parent, but the child will feel sure they are unloved. Children interpret differently to the adult. The adult cannot see that their impatience or persistence causes the child to think that they are an inconvenience to the parent or in some way not wanted, not good enough. These children will cease to bring their problems to the attention of their parents. They will fear the parent's response.

Many children who are constantly criticized will also cease to try, unfortunately this is interpreted by the parent or teacher as obstinacy or idleness when the real reason is probably a fear of more criticism. The easiest way to avoid being criticized is to not begin the task.

We all need to feel we have achieved some level of success in some area of life. If a feeling of success is denied us we cease to aim for it. Learn how to be aware of your child's feelings of achievement in what they do. If they seem pleased with the results so should you. That will encourage them to do even better. Remember that success to your child may mean something totally different than it does to you. If what they do only makes you unhappy or impatient they will stop trying. If their school or other work is causing you or the teacher anger or impatience, they will stop doing it.

To a child, success is pleasing the parent

DIDN'T LIKE IT ANYWAY

It's wet outside, the children are running around the house and you've lost your voice trying to quiet them down.

Then, 'CRASH'.

'On no,' you think, 'what now?'

The crash is proceeded by a deathly quiet. Another bad omen. You enter the lounge and your three kids are all looking like statuettes as if time has stopped and they've been caught in it. No one moves, you look around and then you see it, your favorite ornament in pieces on the floor.

You don't know whether to scream or cry and then you catch sight of the little one, who has broken out of the time lock, trying to sneak out of the door. "You come back here!" you manage to find the strength to speak, and then...

Ok, what are you going to do? Now is your big moment, you have center stage and your audience hanging on your every word and movement. The old saying of 'flight or fight' being very high on their list of priorities right now.

The one thing you don't do is lash out. Stay calm, that will keep your audience off balance. Neither must you accusingly ask, 'which one of you did this?' That question, which they are expecting will turn them against each other and though that might be good tactics in the war games played by generals, it has no place in your home. When this little problem has passed we want harmony to resume; even noisy harmony is better than resentment.

Before this whole episode gets out of proportion to its importance let's consider what is lost and what might be added to that loss if you lose your cool. The situation now is a broken piece of china which nothing will restore and is with every second becoming an incident of the past. You also have three frightened children; not frightened of what they have done, but frightened of your reaction. We now have anticipation of hurt over something which was an accident and in the past anyway. Do you want your children to be scared of you? Can you see the fear in their eyes? Not a very nice feeling is it. Now is your big moment to get a standing ovation from your audience. I suggest the following tactic.

"Ok, clear this lot up and then decide between yourselves what you are going to replace it with. Let me have your answer by tonight."

Then walk out leaving them to clean up the mess and argue between themselves who was to blame and what they are going to buy or give of their own to replace it. One thing you can be certain of, the rest of the day will be quieter and you will have become their heroine or hero. You will have become someone whom it is safe to talk to if they make mistakes. You will be someone whom they are not afraid to tell the truth to because you didn't over react and they will have no need to lie if they ever do anything wrong because they know you will understand.

A frightened child learns to lie to avoid your anger.

So you lost a $200 ornament or something that was your grandmother's and it's going to be replaced with something of less value, but when they come to you with the treasure they have bought or found, the feeling in your heart as they present the replacement with loving smiles will make the replacement a thousand times more valuable than the one you lost and the lesson will have been learned.

Children are more precious than family ornaments.

Reminders
Fear

Adults should protect children from fear.

It is a responsibility of parents to provide a safe, secure haven for their children.

Children are born with a desire to love and be loved, to please and be accepted.

Nothing gives a child greater joy than being able to do something for a parent.

Never find fault with a child just because they are unable to do what you do or as fast as you do it.

Continued and unnecessary criticism causes a halt in effort, because of fear of further criticism.

Children have no desire to make their parents unhappy and the thought of doing so causes fear.

Anyone who puts fear into the heart of another is a menace to society.

Those with love in their hearts never use fear to coerce.

Teasing is funny to the childish adult and fearful to the suffering child and diminishes confidence and self respect.

If a child feels it has to please the parent, it feels unloved.

Fear

Children interpret differently to the adult. It is your responsibility to understand them, it is not their responsibility to understand you.

Impatience creates fear and uncertainty.

All children need to feel they have achieved some level of success in some area of life. Comparison causes fear, robbing the child of ambition and self respect.

You are controlling with guilt when children lack enough self esteem to put their own interests first.

Learn how to be aware of your child's feelings of achievement in what interests them.

Success to the child may mean something totally different to you. Live in their happiness.

To a child success is pleasing the parent.
Let them choose how.

A frightened child learns to lie to avoid your anger.

Children are more precious than family ornaments.

CHAPTER 13

INDEPENDENCE

INDEPENDENCE IS SHARED DEPENDENCE

The greatest gift that any parent can give a child after love is independence. The only purpose the parent has in a child's life is to guide them through their memorable years in an atmosphere of loving security so that the infant can reach a state of confident, happy independence at the emotional age of maturity. The child is not there to satisfy the parents need for purpose or love. The parent is there to guide and guard the child's love and happiness into independence.

Any child who is restricted by a parent's need to satisfy their own needs and ambitions through the child, will have failed in their duty to allow a unique human being entrusted to their care to be confident enough to walk its own path.

Children who grow and learn in an atmosphere of freedom, love, responsibility and happiness will stay within the community of the family. Far better they stay by choice than in an atmosphere of intimidation or because they lack the confidence to be their own person. Independence for many has to be taught and in these times of plenty there is often no need to

reach out for independence. The adoring, loving, often controlling parent providing all the child's needs innocently, sometimes
deliberately, prevents the grown child from reaching out into life
to learn and grow by their own mistakes and successes.

Adults cannot learn a child's mistakes for them.

Life was never meant to be a journey of unlimited success
and ease. The very nature of experience means there will be
mistakes. It is the ability to conquer past mistakes and overcome disappointments and failure that make the human spirit
such a unique and individual being. Guiding the growing child
into independence, however, is not an easy task as the last few
pages have shown.

Independence of thought and action have to be taught and
given. It is far too easy for many youngsters to take the easy
path and let the parents do all the thinking for them and of course,
parents wanting to limit all risks for their children often fall into
the trap of providing everything from financial to intellectual
security. The risk in this is that the child who is not taught
independence will become a follower, allowing those who learn
independence early to become their leaders. Not being taught an
independent way of thinking the followers are easily led into all
sorts of wrong thinking.

Many parents are at a loss to understand why their loving,
caring child left home to go to college to return some months

later with a completely different attitude or set of values to those they left with. They wonder, when did we go wrong? For the answer to this we have to go back to the early learning years.

Children, or most of them, have to be taught how to think and do for themselves. If the parent is willing and able to do and think for them the child will usually offer little resistance. Teaching children to think for themselves begins at a very early age. Most children ask questions not because they are interested in the answer but because it causes the parent to focus attention on them and in that attention is a transfer of energy. Children need energy for survival as any tired parent will tell you and until you teach them to think independently they will be a continuous drain on your resources.

Every time a child asks a question don't give the answer immediately. Ask the child to answer its own question with remarks such as 'why do you think its.......'. Allow the child 2 or 3 attempts, if at the third attempt they haven't come up with the right solution answer the question for them. It will not be long before the child is answering its own questions with such comments as 'Has it stopped working because.......'. Such a child will soon learn to think for itself and begin to reason out what is best for its own life and happiness without blindly listening to the advice of others. The independently thinking child will also become its own energy center and not be a drain on other members of the family.

Independence

It is impossible to outline every situation which might restrict a child's walk into independence. What might cause fear in one child will have no impact at all on another child. For this reason any parent must be aware of their children's development and sensitivities. No therapist can tell you what you should or shouldn't do as every situation is different. No standard set of rules or programs will work because your child is unique and the relationships between the members of your family are unique.

All children have special needs, unique needs to ensure they feel loved, appreciated and accepted in the way they choose to love you.

OOPS, SORRY DADDY!

The phone rings. 'Who could that be?' you think, the kids are out enjoying themselves and you have decided to stay home for the evening. Not that you could do much else when your daughter smiled sweetly and asked if she could have the car.

You make for the phone.

"Hi Daddy"

It takes a little while for your brain to click into gear. "Who's that?"

"Daddy, it's me, your daughter, Penny."

"Oh, you run out of money all ready?" you joke.

"You love me, don't you Daddy?"

"Of course I do, what sort of a question is that?"

173

A Helping Hand

"You really love me lots, don't you Daddy?"

Now you are fully awake. If it was your attention she wanted, she succeeded. In the space of a few seconds you have thought of every possible problem your little sweetheart could have gotten herself into, processed it and thought, 'I'll kill him!'

"You love me more than anything in the world, don't you Daddy?"

"Of course I do," you say exasperated. You take a big gulp of air, brace yourself and wait for whatever is coming.

"You love me more than that silly old car, don't you Daddy?"

"That silly old car," you sputter, "is my new BMW."

"I know, Daddy, but it's only a lump of metal, isn't it?"

You go quiet, knowing it's only a lump of metal now.

This is the moment in the life of you and your child when you let her or him know how much you love and trust them, or when you take over and both the love and trust you have always claimed to have disappears into thin air.

If you follow the path of love and trust, the conversation will proceed something like this:

"Daddy, you still there?"

"Sorry honey, just felt a bit sick for a moment. You two ok?"

"Sure, Daddy, we are fine; car is beyond help, though"

"So long as you are safe. What happened?"

"Some drunk driver rammed us in the side and I think your car is unlikely to move on its own again."

"Have you called the cops?"

"Yes, that's all taken care of."

"That's good, do you need me to come over, bring you home or help in any way?"

"Thanks, Daddy, nice to know you are there, but I can handle it."

"Ok, Penny, call the garage and get them to clean up the mess and if you need me I'll be here by the phone. As long as you are OK, we can always get another car. As you say, it's only a lump of metal." You gulp again.

That is the right way to deal with the situation. No panic, no third degree questioning, no threatening or offensive language about what you will do to the other guy. No rushing down to the scene of the accident to take over.

This is total love and trust in your children's ability to look after themselves. There is very little that you could do anyway. Of course, if you have brought them up to be totally dependent on you, you will now be dealing with screaming, hysterical children who need you to be there to organize everything for them. After all, the screaming hysteria is only what they will have learned from you. If you rage when there is a problem so will they. The fear they feel is caused by what they expect of you, not by what has taken place.

Children are more capable of self determination than
most parents give them credit for.

Independence, of course, necessitates a sense of responsibility and far too many children are protected from the need to care for or consider others. Many of them are even shielded from the responsibility of looking after their own pets with mother or father taking the dog for walks, feeding the rabbit or cleaning the stable if your child is lucky enough to have a pony. Contrary to popular belief children of all ages desire responsibility. It gives them a feeling of being trusted and independent. To be trusted with responsibility and see a parent's proud smile at their early efforts to master life is a fulfilling moment in a child's life. The more responsibility they are given within their abilities and not be overwhelmed, the greater their self confidence and self respect will be.

Once having taken responsibility for a situation such as being given the puppy or kitten they have always wanted, the child should be encouraged to continue the responsibility after the initial enthusiasm has worn off. The Fun-loving type, particularly, will tire easily of the duty and leave the responsibility to others for continuing what they started. The rules need to be in place before the wished for responsibility is granted. It needs to be explained that if they become responsible for animals of any sort that this is something that will have to continue throughout the animal's life. Mother, father or some other family member is not going to take over when the excitement or glamor has worn away.

I believe the rules should be that if a pet is the responsibility, the child must attend to the pet's needs before their own. That the dog, cat or whatever is fed and exercised before the child has breakfast and that on returning home the pet's needs are again attended to before the child is allowed to settle into their own needs or wants. Isn't that what you, having become a parent, have decided to do? For as long as your child needs you, your own needs will take second place to theirs.

Assuming responsibility for a life is an awesome commitment and is not to be taken lightly. Whether animal or child, it doesn't matter if the life that has become dependent upon your loving care and attention is a little animal or a child, life is of God and therefore all life is precious and we have a responsibility to ensure that for as long as that life is dependent upon our love and understanding we must give of our love, unconditionally, to ensure their happiness and contentment.

If the life in our care is a child, we have a responsibility to help them become happy, fulfilled, independent people whose trust in our love for their well being is something they are proud to learn and pass on to their children.

Our children don't belong to us. We have borrowed them from God until they are ready, through loving independence, to walk with Him on their own.

Look for your children's happiness,
not their potential,
because it is in their happiness
that you will find their potential.

Reminders
Independence

The greatest gift any parent can give a child after love, is independence.

The only purpose the parent has is to guide the child with love into a happy future.

The child is not there to satisfy the parents need for purpose.

Any parent who restricts a child in reaching out for their own destiny will have failed in their duty towards that child.

If there is anything that should be placed above the reach of another human being, it is a child's self respect.

Adults cannot learn a child's mistakes for them.

Children who are not given or taught independence will become followers of children who were guided in their own destiny.

Young children ask questions to cause parents to focus attention and therefore energy on them.

All children have special needs, unique needs to insure they feel loved, appreciated and accepted in the way they choose to love you.

Children are more capable of self determination than most parents give them credit for.

A Helping Hand

POPULAR WORKS
BY
MALCOLM S. SOUTHWOOD

Books

Teach Me How To Love, So I Can Heal. This delightful book is a prescription for living life in perfect attitude, health, and awareness. It was written because a young woman named Chrissie wanted to heal herself and learn more about spiritual love and healing. She asked many of the questions the rest of us would like to ask. This now popular book is a must for everyone who wants to live happily and healthfully and learn how to help others heal themselves from the inside out.

The Healing Experience. Anyone who is interested in learning about spiritual healing will want to read this book more than once. Mr. Southwood shares what he has learned as a full-time healing practitioner and presents many case histories of spiritual healing. This book dissolves many of the mysteries of healing by explaining common sense approaches to spiritual healing and why they work. This book is essential reading for those who are interested in understanding themselves and others.

The Challenge. Are we merely the helpless victims of suffering, confusion, and a capricious fate? This book argues that, on the contrary, each of us possesses, through the energy vibrations of thought, the key to our own well-being, to healing ourselves and others, and to comprehending the nature of existence.

The Ten Great Laws. In this booklet, Mr. Southwood reinterprets The Ten Commandments for practical use in the present age.

Audio Cassette Tapes

In My Silence, Tape One. Dedicated to those going through difficult times, it is softly spoken to comfort and guide listeners into their silence, where all things are known.

Spiritual Healing, Tape Two. A soothing tape that logically explains healing and how to use it in everyday life.

The Impact of Love, Tape Three. This is a very popular tape. Mr. Southwood shares messages about healing through unconditional love and guides the listener through healing exercises.

The Ten Great Laws, Tape Four. Mr. Southwood reinterprets the Biblical sacred laws as they relate to our present world.

The Aura of Love, Tape Five. This tape describes unconditional Love and how it benefits those who demonstrate it and those who are the recipients of it. This tape is a must for anyone who considers themselves to be on a spiritual path